THIS BOOK IS BROKEN

THIS

STUART BERMAN

BOO

BRO

KIS

KEN

A
BROKEN SOCIAL SCENE
STORY

ANANSI

THIS EDITION PUBLISHED IN 2009 BY
HOUSE OF ANANSI PRESS INC.
110 SPADINA AVENUE, SUITE 801
TORONTO, ON, M5V 2K4
TEL. 416-363-4343
FAX 416-363-1017
WWW.ANANSI.CA

DISTRIBUTED IN CANADA BY   DISTRIBUTED IN THE UNITED STATES BY
HARPERCOLLINS CANADA LTD.   PUBLISHERS GROUP WEST
1995 MARKHAM ROAD   1700 FOURTH STREET
SCARBOROUGH, ON, M1B 5M8   BERKELEY, CA 94710
TOLL FREE TEL. 1-800-387-0117   TOLL FREE TEL. 1-800-788-3123

HOUSE OF ANANSI PRESS IS COMMITTED TO PROTECTING OUR NATURAL ENVIRONMENT.
AS PART OF OUR EFFORTS, THIS BOOK IS PRINTED ON PAPER THAT CONTAINS 60%
POST-CONSUMER RECYCLED FIBRES, IS ACID-FREE, AND IS PROCESSED CHLORINE-FREE.

13 12 11 10 09   1 2 3 4 5

LIBRARY AND ARCHIVES CANADA CATALOGUING IN PUBLICATION

BERMAN, STUART
    THIS BOOK IS BROKEN : A BROKEN SOCIAL SCENE STORY / STUART
BERMAN.

ISBN 978-0-88784-228-3 (BOUND).—ISBN 978-0-88784-796-7 (PBK.)

    1. BROKEN SOCIAL SCENE (MUSICAL GROUP). 2. ROCK MUSICIANS—
CANADA—BIOGRAPHY. I. TITLE. II. TITLE: BROKEN SOCIAL SCENE STORY.

ML421.B867B52 2009   782.42166092'2   C2008-901058-2

LIBRARY OF CONGRESS CONTROL NUMBER: 2008922788

 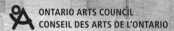

Canada Council
for the Arts

ONTARIO ARTS COUNCIL
CONSEIL DES ARTS DE L'ONTARIO

WE ACKNOWLEDGE FOR THEIR FINANCIAL SUPPORT OF OUR PUBLISHING PROGRAM
THE CANADA COUNCIL FOR THE ARTS, THE ONTARIO ARTS COUNCIL, AND THE GOVERNMENT
OF CANADA THROUGH THE BOOK PUBLISHING INDUSTRY DEVELOPMENT PROGRAM (BPIDP).

COVER ART AND DESIGN: BILL DOUGLAS AT THE BANG
TEXT DESIGN, TAPE COLLAGES, AND TYPESETTING: BILL DOUGLAS AT THE BANG

PRINTED AND BOUND IN CHINA

CONTENTS

WEBSTER HALL
BROKEN SOCIAL
SCENE PLAYS
KEVIN DREW S SPIRIT IF

1 The Cause
2 Charles Song
3 C - Song
4 Pacific theme
5 Wrong side
6 Jimmy & the photo call
7 Fuzz /Song
8 Emily New Song
9 it's all gonna break
10 Looks Like the Sun
11 Backyards
12 ~~the stuck~~
   grateful dead

e wisdom
OF NO Escape

Pema Chodron

C Song

Jimmy & the Photo Call

the shoe

djaN 12.02

01 . 12 . 02

BROKEn
sociaL
sCene

open FOR

MORE ✶ PLASTiC

MORE ✶ PLASTiC

more plastic

more

lullabye

Jimmy

Pcc

7/4

Fireyed

Cause

Stars

Handjobs

Anthems

Hotel

Almost

1B1

Major Fast

CAST LIST

The majority of the interviews featured in this book were conducted between June and December 2007; some quotes were sourced from past interviews I conducted between 2001 and 2007 for Eye Weekly, Magnet, TORO, *and* Report on Business *magazine.*

OHAD BENCHETRIT is a founding member of Do Make Say Think. He is also a part-time member of Broken Social Scene and co-produced Kevin Drew's 2007 solo album *Spirit If* . . . .

DAVE "BOOKIE" BOOKMAN has been an on-air personality at Toronto alternative rock station 102.1 The Edge (formerly CFNY) since 1991.

NADIN BRENDEL has tour-managed Broken Social Scene in Europe since 2004. Her booking agency, Mikrokultur, is based in Berlin, Germany.

JONATHAN BUNCE is a co-founder of the Wavelength concert series and a veteran of many late, great Toronto indie-rock bands, including Secret Agent, Kid Sniper, Currently in These United States, and Republic of Safety.

TYLER CLARK BURKE is a Toronto-based visual artist and was a co-founder of Three Gut Records.

TORQUIL CAMPBELL is a singer for Stars.

BRENDAN "THE CHAMP" CANNING is the co-founder of Broken Social Scene and a former member of hHead, By Divine Right, Valley of the Giants, Len, Spookey Ruben, and Blurtonia. He released his first solo album, *Something for All of Us*, in 2008.

STEPHEN CHUNG is a Toronto-based photographer and videographer who filmed many of Broken Social Scene's early gigs. He is currently working on a Broken Social Scene documentary.

JASON COLLETT is a Toronto-based singer/songwriter and member of Broken Social Scene. He is a former member of Ursula and also released two albums in the late 1990s under the name Bird.

EVAN CRANLEY is a member of Broken Social Scene and Stars.

JOHN CROSSINGHAM plays guitar and drums in Broken Social Scene and is a founding member of indie-rock trio Raising the Fawn.

KEVIN DREW is the co-founder of Broken Social Scene and K.C. Accidental. In 2007, he released his first solo album on Arts & Crafts Records, *Spirit If* . . . .

JOE ENGLISH is the founder of Toronto experimental-music label Noise Factory Records.

LESLIE FEIST is a member of Broken Social Scene. She has also released three solo albums, including 2004's Juno award–winning *Let It Die* and 2007's Grammy-nominated *The Reminder*. She is a former member of Noah's Arkweld, By Divine Right, and Royal City and has collaborated with Peaches and Chilly Gonzales.

GENTLEMAN REG is a Toronto singer/songwriter who released three albums for Three Gut Records and is a former member of The Hidden Cameras.

JOEL GIBB is the founding member of "gay folk church music" ensemble The Hidden Cameras.

JO-ANN GOLDSMITH was a part-time trumpet player for Broken Social Scene.

EMILY HAINES is a member of Broken Social Scene and the singer/keyboardist for Metric. In 2006, she released a solo album, *Knives Don't Have Your Back*, under the name Emily Haines & the Soft Skeleton, followed by an EP, *What Is Free to a Good Home?*, in 2007.

HAYDEN is a Toronto singer/songwriter whose 1995 debut, *Everything I Long For*, was one of the most acclaimed Canadian independent releases of the 1990s. He continues to release music through his own Hardwood Records label.

JORIS JARSKY is a Toronto-based actor whose film credits include *Blindness* and *The Incredible Hulk*. He attended the Etobicoke School of the Arts with Kevin Drew.

DANKO JONES is the front man for his eponymous garage-rock band and a former roommate of Brendan Canning.

SCOTT KANNBERG A.K.A. SPIRAL STAIRS was a founding member of Stockton, California–based 1990s indie-rock icons Pavement. He continues to record as Preston School of Industry.

MARTY KINACK has been Broken Social Scene's sound man since 2003. He is a former member of Transistor Sound and Lighting Co. and has produced albums for Sarah Harmer.

K-OS is a Toronto-based MC who has released three albums — *Exit*, *Joyful Rebellion*, and *Atlantis: Hymns for the Disco* — to critical and commercial acclaim.

STEVE LAMBKE is a singer/guitarist for Constantines.

MURRAY LIGHTBURN is the front man for Montreal art-pop ensemble The Dears.

LISA LOBSINGER joined Broken Social Scene in 2005 as a touring singer. She also performs with the Calgary-based band Reverie Sound Revue.

J MASCIS is the singer/guitarist and sole constant member of legendary Amherst, Massachusetts–based indie-rock trio Dinosaur Jr.

YVONNE MATSELL is the former booker at Toronto clubs the Ultrasound, the Reverb, and Ted's Wrecking Yard. She currently books at the El Mocambo.

AMY MILLAN is a member of Broken Social Scene and Stars. She released a solo album, *Honey from the Tombs*, on Arts & Crafts in 2006.

CHRISTOPHER MILLS is a Toronto-based filmmaker who directed Broken Social Scene's first video, "Stars and Sons." He has also directed videos for Interpol and Modest Mouse.

NOAH MINTZ was a founding member of hHead with Brendan Canning. He has mastered every Broken Social Scene album to date, and continues to perform as Noah's Arkweld.

GORDON MOAKES is the bassist for London, U.K.–based post-punk quartet Bloc Party.

LISA MORAN is the former head of Three Gut Records. In 2006, she relocated to Brooklyn, New York, to join Sufjan Stevens's management team.

DAVE NEWFELD produced Broken Social Scene's *You Forgot It In People* (2002) and *Broken Social Scene* (2005), as well as Apostle of Hustle's *Folkloric Feel* (2004). In 2007, he produced albums for Welsh bands Super Furry Animals and Los Campesinos!

JULIE PENNER plays violin for Broken Social Scene, Do Make Say Think, and FemBots.

JUSTIN PEROFF is the drummer for Broken Social Scene. He also DJs and promotes parties under the alias Juicetan.

BILL PRIDDLE is a "founding non-member" of Broken Social Scene and a former member of Treble Charger. He recently recorded his first solo album, *Hold Me on Tight*.

JEFFREY REMEDIOS worked for six years at Virgin Music Canada, eventually becoming the company's director of promotions. Upon leaving the label in 2002, he formed Arts & Crafts Records with his former roommate Kevin Drew.

JAMES SHAW is a member of Broken Social Scene and the guitarist for Metric.

CHARLES SPEARIN is a member of Broken Social Scene and a founding member of Do Make Say Think and K.C. Accidental. He co-produced Kevin Drew's *Spirit If . . .* with Ohad Benchetrit.

GEORGE VALE is a Toronto-based video director and co-founder of the Experimental Parachute Moment filmmaking collective with Kevin Drew. His credits include the videos for "Almost Crimes," "Cause = Time," "Fire Eye'd Boy," and Feist's "Mushaboom."

BRY WEBB is the singer/guitarist for Constantines.

ANDREW WHITEMAN is a guitarist for Broken Social Scene. He also performs as the Apostle of Hustle and is a former member of The Bourbon Tabernacle Choir and Que Vida.

ERIC YEALLAND is a Toronto-based video director and reggae DJ, and is also one of the co-owners of popular Queen Street drinking establishment The Beaconsfield.

FOREWORD

SEPTEMBER 2009 will mark the tenth anniversary of when Kevin Drew and I began recording what would become *Feel Good Lost*, Broken Social Scene's debut album. If we were any good at planning ahead, I'm sure we would have had a tenth anniversary album release prepared, or a deluxe re-issue with bonus tracks already in the can. But because this band has always followed its natural path, it's hard to predict with any certainty what's going to happen to us next.

This uncertainty has been a blessing and a curse for as long as we have been a touring ensemble, one that has taken its show from Halifax to Chicago to Mexico City to Moscow. And this uncertainty has frustrated (and will continue to frustrate, I'm sure) girlfriends, wives, parents, fans, managers, label peeps, agents, bandmates, producers, video directors, and, lest we forget, the press — but they all stick around for some reason. Probably because everyone likes a good dramatic epic, playing out in the saga that is our lives . . . and maybe in the music.

We are friends first, then bandmates. That has always been our ethos, and is what allows us to keep our sanity. What we created together in Toronto is a most wonderful thing to be a part of. It can keep you up at night, but it will get your ass out of bed in the morning too.

BRENDAN CANNING
TORONTO, ONTARIO
AUGUST 19, 2008 2:22 A.M.

INTRODUCTION

OK, I'LL COME CLEAN. BROKEN SOCIAL SCENE ARE FRIENDS. I'VE GOTTEN DRUNK WITH THEM, PASSED OUT ON THEIR COUCHES, BEEN TO SOME OF THEIR WEDDINGS; THEY'VE EVEN HELPED ME MOVE.

These were the opening lines of my five-star review of Broken Social Scene's breakthrough album, *You Forgot It In People*, which ran in the October 11, 2002, edition of *Eye Weekly*. It was a somewhat apologetic preamble to awarding a perfect score to a band that, at the time, was completely unknown outside of Toronto indie-music circles. But my belief in that album overpowered any instinct to respect the traditional distance between critic and subject — Broken Social Scene was a conflict of interest worth fighting for.

And really, there was nothing to worry about: *You Forgot It In People* would transform Broken Social Scene from a local secret to global emissaries for the Toronto indie-rock community. But what seemed like a sudden, unforeseen success to the rest of the world was really the climax to a narrative that began a decade before. More than an assemblage of many musicians, Broken Social Scene is the culmination of ten years of false starts, missed opportunities, chance meetings, demographic trends, technological breakthroughs, industry upheavals, and paradigm shifts — all of which created the conditions for a revolving-door Toronto collective to become not just a concert-hall-filling phenomenon but also an unlikely model for surviving and thriving in a troubled, major-label-dominated music industry that now seems more interested in suing their customers than serving them.

My own unsuspecting induction into this universe came in the spring of 1997 at Toronto club Lee's Palace, where, as an associate arts editor for University of Toronto's *Varsity* newspaper, I first met Jeffrey Remedios — then a Virgin/EMI Music Canada campus media rep with whom I had previously interacted over the phone. Playing that night at Lee's were space-rock jammers Do Make Say Think and recent EMI signees King Cobb Steelie. The former are an instrumental ensemble who would go on to play an integral role in Broken Social Scene's formation. The latter were a Toronto (via Guelph) polyrhythmic dub-rock band whose history typified that of fellow indie bands in the 1990s: release a couple of promising records through small local imprints; pique the interest of a Canadian major label hoping to cash in on the post-Nirvana alternative rock boom; and then count your losses as that ineffective major label fails to get you onto increasingly regimented Canadian commercial radio playlists or facilitate your entry into the tough U.S. touring market.

During a Saturday night party-hop with Remedios in April 1998, I met Brendan Canning, a local musician who had already played out a variation of the aforementioned script with grunge hopefuls-turned-also-rans hHead. Though Canning still played bass regularly with several bands (By Divine Right, Spookey Ruben, and Len), his interest in indie-rock was waning. The first time we met, he was DJing house music at an after-hours loft party — a natural career change at a time when rock clubs were closing down, or switching their programming to DJ dance nights in order to capitalize on the emergent electronica trend. Our initial meeting amounted to just a handshake and a wave, but I'd get to know Canning much better in the fall of 1999, when I moved into the middle apartment of a Gladstone Avenue triplex above Remedios (who tipped me off to the vacancy). My two new roommates, Judy Faulds and Grace Lutsch, happened to be Canning's best friend and second cousin, respectively, a circumstance that quickly clued me in to the fact that Brendan Canning knows *everybody*.

Canning's regular visits to our apartment would become even more frequent the following year, when Remedios acquired a new roommate: Kevin Drew, who was a

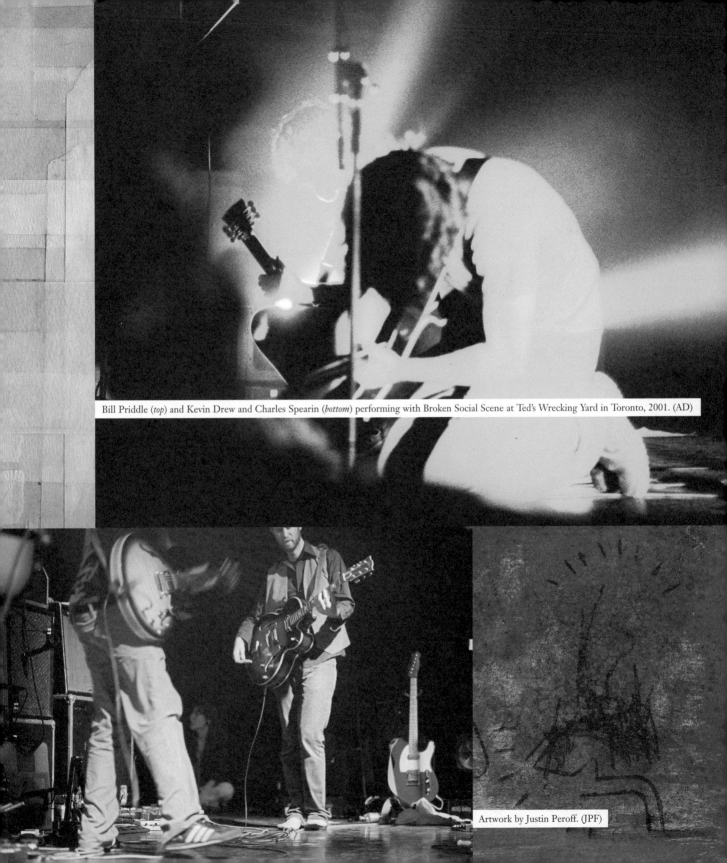

Bill Priddle (*top*) and Kevin Drew and Charles Spearin (*bottom*) performing with Broken Social Scene at Ted's Wrecking Yard in Toronto, 2001. (AD)

Artwork by Justin Peroff. (JPF)

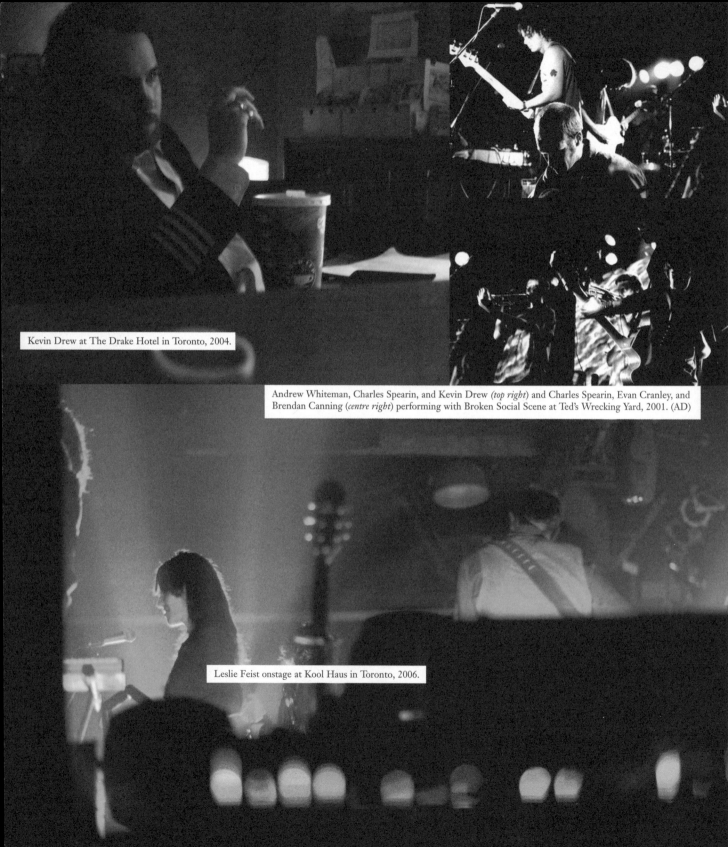

Kevin Drew at The Drake Hotel in Toronto, 2004.

Andrew Whiteman, Charles Spearin, and Kevin Drew *(top right)* and Charles Spearin, Evan Cranley, and Brendan Canning *(centre right)* performing with Broken Social Scene at Ted's Wrecking Yard, 2001. (AD)

Leslie Feist onstage at Kool Haus in Toronto, 2006.

member of instrumental ambient-rock band K.C. Accidental with Do Make Say Think's Charles Spearin. While I was blasting my Trail of Dead records upstairs, Drew and Canning were in the apartment below plotting Broken Social Scene's transformation from basement recording project into a living, breathing live band. Meanwhile, Drew, a fiercely passionate indie-rock idealist, was inspiring Remedios — who by that point had quickly risen to the post of Virgin's national publicity director — to question his place in a major-label system that was moving ever more toward formulaic, radio-ready pop music in response to the encroaching threat of Internet file-sharing.

A month before Broken Social Scene's debut album, *Feel Good Lost*, was released, Canning and Drew booked a show at College Street club Ted's Wrecking Yard (R.I.P.) in January 2001. But this was no CD-release gig; instead of performing the low-key, languid instrumentals heard on *Feel Good Lost*, Drew and Canning opened the stage to a host of friends — K.C. Accidental drummer Justin Peroff, former By Divine Right member Leslie Feist, and guitarist Andrew Whiteman (a.k.a. the Apostle of Hustle) — and performed a set of loosely structured songs that blurred the lines between psychedelia, indie-rock, dub reggae, and soul. It's no coincidence that the emergence of Broken Social Scene as an amorphous onstage entity — accumulating fans gig by gig through their unpredictable, unwieldy nature — happened around the same time Drew moved out of Remedios's Gladstone apartment and into a house with his future wife, Jo-Ann Goldsmith. The new home not only provided Broken Social Scene with a basement jam space in which to experiment with new song ideas — many of which formed the basis for *You Forgot It In People* — but also a cozy living room for late-night gatherings.

And really, watching Broken Social Scene at Ted's Wrecking Yard was no different from hanging out with them in the living room: you never knew who was going to turn up or what was going to happen. Just as a song like "Anthems for a Seventeen-Year-Old Girl" could begin as a twee lullaby and blossom into a climactic crescendo, a casual invite to Kev and Jo's for a glass of wine on a Tuesday night could, within an hour, turn into an impromptu dinner party for thirty that would end in living-room slow dances — even if all the ladies were actually outside smoking in the backyard.

(I've always maintained that Kevin Drew is the guy who made it okay for heterosexual Toronto indie-rock boys to hug one another.) Every show Broken Social Scene played in 2001 was completely different from the one before. Sometimes James Shaw and Emily Haines were on stage, other times you saw Stars' Torquil Campbell and Amy Millan; sometimes Charles Spearin of Do Make Say Think and Evan Cranley of Stars were playing guitar, other times they were blowing horns; sometimes the band hid behind a screen of psychedelic projections, other times they were coaxing the crowd into clapping along. But what was happening in the living room and in the basement and on the stage was just a microcosm of a prevailing communal ethic that was reinvigorating Toronto's indie music scene: upstart labels like Three Gut Records, weekly concert series like Wavelength and Radio Mondays, and bands like The Hidden Cameras and Constantines were forging a new participatory culture inside and outside of Toronto clubs, staging concerts in warehouse lofts, galleries, and churches and cross-pollinating with local art, activist, and queer communities. Within this open environment, the primary motivation for playing music was not a contract but simply contact: shared ideas, collaborations, audience interaction. (As Torquil Campbell of Stars is fond of saying, "We should do as the hippies did, only dress better.")

Broken Social Scene spent the better part of 2002 in Dave Newfeld's Stars and Sons studios, harnessing those basement jams and Ted's Wrecking Yard experiences into pristine pop songs that were diverse in form but united by a shared emotional response. Upon its release that October, *You Forgot It In People* became the exclamation mark for a moment in time when — amid looming news-ticker threats of SARS epidemics and Iraq-War sequels — the Toronto indie-rock community felt like a self-sufficient utopian city-state where George Bush couldn't hurt us, the lines separating performer and audience were dissolved, and, most important, the tunes were really good.

Shortly after the release of *You Forgot It In People*, Drew confessed he wasn't sure how such an eclectic album would be received. He feared Broken Social Scene had created a scattershot compilation of styles — noisy indie-rock anthems, dub-influenced instrumentals, ambient electronic pieces, loungey surf themes, bossa nova balladry — instead of a coherent body of work. What he didn't realize at the time was that, with

Emily Haines singing lead vocals at a Broken Social Scene concert at Ted's Wrecking Yard, 2001. (AD)

Charles Spearin (*left and right*) performing at The Drake Hotel in Toronto, 2004.

the advent of iPod Shuffles, MySpace band pages, and MP3 blogs, this sense of randomness would come to define our current generation's listening habits, and that the band's burgeoning international fan base was already in the process of being built, one peer-to-peer download at a time. If Broken Social Scene albums sound like compilations, it's because the band members are an amalgam themselves: their myriad solo careers and satellite bands — Stars, Metric, Feist, Apostle of Hustle, Do Make Say Think, Raising the Fawn, Jason Collett — each represent discrete, disparate components of the band's wall of sound.

All of these artists predated the formation of Broken Social Scene, but their profiles were raised considerably through their association with the band and (with a few exceptions) its label, Arts & Crafts. Combining Drew's indie-schooled values with Remedios's major-label-bred marketing savvy, Arts & Crafts helped forge a new middle tier within the Canadian music industry's binary mainstream/underground parameters, showing that independent artists need not starve or sign their lives away. And in the process, both band and label have helped establish Toronto as a thriving indie music locus in the eyes of an international music industry and the media that once ignored it.

However, the history documented over the following pages shows that the traditional definition of a music scene is actually outmoded — that the division between under- and above-ground is ultimately arbitrary. In their past and present lives, the members of Broken Social Scene have toured hockey arenas with The Tragically Hip; traded potty-mouthed raps with Peaches; song-doctored hit singles for blues rockers Big Sugar; recorded with indie-rock icons (Dinosaur Jr.'s J Mascis, Pavement's Scott Kannberg), Top-40 rappers (k-os), and Canadian pop stars (Tom Cochrane) alike. Their music has been featured in Oscar-nominated Ryan Gosling vehicles and Sigourney Weaver art-house films, while 2007 saw Feist achieve the ultimate measure of pop-culture ubiquity — not the four Grammy nominations, but the iPod commercial featuring her hit single "1234."

Whatever shape Broken Social Scene takes from here on could turn out to be something quite different from the one that created the band's first three albums and the one documented in this book. Because, in effect, the band's success is also its curse:

Brendan Canning at the Hammerstein Ballroom, New York City, 2004. (SH)

Leslie Feist performing at The Drake Hotel in Toronto, 2004.

Poster for a show at Ted's Wrecking Yard, 2001. (JPF)

the careers of individual members and auxiliary bands have been catapulted to such a level of activity and acclaim that they have less time to tend to the mothership. In September 2007, Kevin Drew released his first solo album, *Spirit If . . .* , which was followed by the summer 2008 release of Brendan Canning's solo album *Something for All of Us*. They toured both records under the name Broken Social Scene, with reconstituted lineups that suggest the band has entered a new phase — the circus-like collective downsized into a more functional formation.

But even if some of its most visible members (Feist, Emily Haines, Jason Collett) are off attending to their own careers and seem less present in the band's current identity, my time observing Broken Social Scene — both as a writer and as a friend — has taught me that this band exists in a state of perpetual temporariness, in a continued history comprised of passing phases. And yet, within their chaotic chronology, a certain truth still holds. It's the same maxim that ended my *Eye Weekly* review from 2002: "This is for you as much as it is for them. Because, hey, we're all friends here." Even if you now need a backstage pass to say hi to them after the show.

STUART BERMAN
TORONTO, MAY 2008

AS BAD AS THEY SEEM

1990s

THE TORONTO INDIE BOOM GOES BUST

TORONTO IS HOME to the head offices of all the Canadian major record labels, which, thanks to the endless cycle of corporate mergers, is an ever-shrinking pool that currently includes Universal Music Canada, Sony BMG Canada, EMI Music Canada, and Warner Music Canada. Regardless of which company name is spelled out on the corporate letterhead, the Canadian majors' modus operandi has remained mostly unchanged since their establishment in the 1960s and '70s: sign commercially viable Canadian artists, build them a domestic audience, then export the most successful ones to their international parent companies for worldwide release — and pray for the best (or at least another Loverboy).

But in the shadows of these monoliths, a grassroots-oriented network of left-of-centre Toronto rock bands emerged in the late 1980s and early 1990s: Change of Heart, the Rheostatics, Lowest of the Low, The Bourbon Tabernacle Choir, King Cobb Steelie, and the Barenaked Ladies, whose handmade first release, 1991's *The Yellow Tape*, would famously go on to sell more than 100,000 copies in Canada and, more important, establish a retail presence for domestic independent music. Inspired by the seismic success of Nirvana south of the border and thriving communities in Halifax and Moncton (spearheaded by Sloan and Eric's Trip, respectively), Toronto's indie-rock culture flourished in the mid-'90s as post-grunge artists like Hayden, Treble Charger, and hHead received heavy rotation on local alternative rock station CFNY. (To underscore their support for the city's music scene, the station also awarded $100,000 to an emergent artist through their annual New Music Search contest.) And for every Toronto indie band that made it onto radio or

MuchMusic, there were countless more operating further underground — like experimental jazz ensemble GUH and noise-rock provocateurs Grasshopper — and building a following through self-released cassettes and shows held in illicit warehouse and basement venues.

But by the late '90s, Toronto was starting to feel like a big city saddled with small-town barriers. Local bands that sold out a Saturday-night show at Lee's Palace really had nowhere else to go. They either got turned back at the border because the Americans didn't care or, if they were crazy enough to tour across Canada in a van, no one knew if anyone would show up at the gigs. (The Internet, of course, had yet to develop into an effective means for disseminating musical information to far-flung locales.) By decade's end, electronic music was stealing indie-rock's headlines, while several key developmental live rooms in Toronto had either shut down (The Ultrasound) or abandoned live music programming for DJ dance nights (Sneaky Dee's). After changing corporate ownership, CFNY rebranded itself 102.1 The Edge and began to resemble a more typical American modern-rock station, playing more pop-punk and nu-metal (or Canadian facsimiles thereof) at the expense of local content and initiatives such as the discontinued New Music Search. The indie-music section at HMV's Yonge Street flagship store — which in the early '90s proudly displayed Change of Heart and hHead records in prominent front-of-store racks — had by 1998 been demoted to the back wall on the store's second floor.

The future members of Broken Social Scene experienced Toronto's indie boom/bust first-hand, either as industry-courted participants (Brendan "the Champ" Canning with hHead, Andrew Whiteman with The Bourbon Tabernacle Choir, Bill Priddle with Treble Charger, Jason Collett with the roots-rock band Ursula and his own solo project, Bird) or as fans observing from the sidelines (Kevin Drew, Justin Peroff, John Crossingham, Charles Spearin). Their experiences in the 1990s were echoed by fellow musicians like Hayden and Danko Jones, show promoters like Yvonne Matsell, CFNY DJ Dave Bookman, and future Arts & Crafts label founder Jeffrey Remedios, who entered the music business through an internship in the Virgin Music Canada publicity department — just in time to watch the industry's house of cards start to collapse.

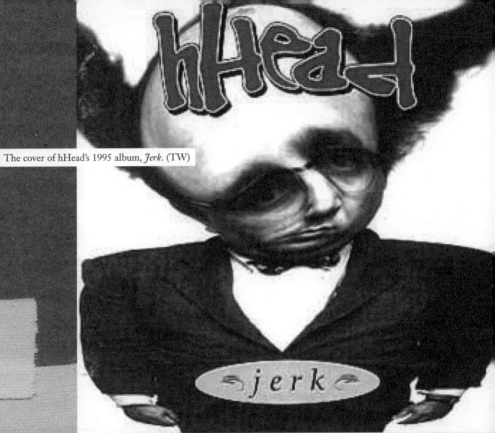

The cover of hHead's 1995 album, *Jerk*. (TW)

Ad for Spookey Ruben with Feist and Danko Jones at Lee's Palace in Toronto, 1999. (SB)

DAVE BOOKMAN_ The initial burst of activity for independent music in Toronto happened with the Barenaked Ladies and the Lowest of the Low — their success was really the local byproduct of the indie movement that had happened in the States and England in the 1980s. Subsequently, you saw the first wave of indie labels like Intrepid Records, who put the first Rheostatics record out. Here in Toronto, we had a great infrastructure set up, from promoters to clubs to radio stations to weeklies that really made the music scene a lot more accessible for people. As far as our station [CFNY] goes, we used to give away $100,000 to an indie band each year. We gave $100,000 to the Barenaked Ladies, we gave $100,000 to hHead and Change of Heart. That was really cool. That was the system working.

JOHN CROSSINGHAM_ It's impossible to separate Broken Social Scene from all the work that was done before, by bands like the Rheostatics, Change of Heart, Sloan, and their whole Murderecords scene. The early '90s was a moment when Canadian indie rock was really proving itself — for the most part, it was only proving itself within the context of its own country, but within Canada, people were listening to a lot of Canadian indie rock. It was great. Even if it wasn't happening around the world, everyone here was like, "I'm just as excited about Hayden and Treble Charger and Hardship Post as I am about any other band."

YVONNE MATSELL_ Lowest of the Low could play every week and pack the place every time — people couldn't miss a show because they loved them. That, for me, represents what music is all about. All of the bands were really strong supporters of each other. The Rheos would be out at a Barenaked Ladies show and vice versa, and whoever was doing really well at that time would put the other band on the bill as the opener.

ANDREW WHITEMAN_ The Bourbon Tabernacle Choir were a total reaction against Wham! and all the '80s shit we hated so much. So instead of embracing the future, we all ran backwards and embraced Curtis Mayfield and Van Morrison. That was my world for five years, but I got bored of that, and then I quit [in 1992]. I had friends feeding me cassette tapes with Public Enemy and Pavement, and those musical influences had been infiltrating my consciousness. I went straight into the indie-rock warehouse scene at King and Dufferin, with bands like GUH, Adventure Playground, Grasshopper, Venus Cures All — we all thought Venus Cures All was going to be the fucking thing.

CHARLES SPEARIN_ I was living with [Do Make Say Think bandmates] Justin Small and James Payment at Albany and Bloor, and we would just go from free music night to free music night: Tuesday night was the Horseshoe, Wednesday night was Lee's Palace. There were tons of bands to see every night, and it didn't cost anything. And it was a great way to meet people who do the same thing. There was all the fertile ground for a music community. I wasn't really a part of it; I was a spectator. But there were a few bands I started going to see a lot, like GUH. They were a big influence on me at that time; they wiped away any pretense of what a band was supposed to be like. Their music was as experimental and playful and serious and hilarious as you wanted it to be.

DANKO JONES_ The definition of indie-rock has changed over the years. Today, with the advent of Pitchfork Media, it's easy for people to assimilate into the scene, whereas ten to fifteen years ago, you really had to go out and find it. We looked at garage-rock bands from the States — they were on tiny labels, but toured a lot and were able to get their name out up north to us. That gave me the inspiration to say, "We can do that."

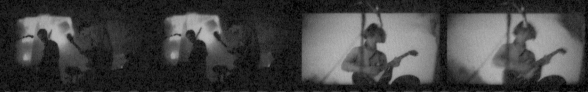

Do Make Say Think concert at the Bloor Cinema in Toronto, 1998. (SK)

The scene at The Mockingbird in Toronto, 1997. (SC)

*HAYDEN_* There was a really lively scene in Toronto at that time, and that stemmed from having all-ages shows at clubs, and the whole East Coast rock explosion — Sub Pop [in Seattle] had signed Eric's Trip — and there were lots of indie labels, like [Hamilton, Ontario's] Sonic Unyon. But I definitely felt that after '98 the enthusiasm died down and almost disappeared for a while. Once a band signed to a Canadian major label, they'd release an album and that would be it: the label put all the money into Canadian promotion, but the bands never seemed to break out of the country. Canadian major labels weren't a good option at the time.

*KEVIN DREW_* Toronto was the major-label town of Canada, and slowly everyone realized that [model] was going nowhere, whether it was with Treble Charger or hHead or Change of Heart — these bands could only reach a certain point. Hayden slipped through that whole scenario because of independence, because he started out by selling 20,000 records on Sonic Unyon alone. He is one of the lucky ones, because he then signed an American major record deal [with Universal Music affiliate Outpost Recordings] that went nowhere, but then a year later that label was cleaning house and they bought him out of his contract, which gave him what is everyone's goal: artistic freedom with a [financially comfortable] life. For me, Hayden in this country is always going to go down as a Leonard Cohen, as a Neil Young, because he was the first one to achieve the independence of doing what he needed through a major-label system that was just about to die.

*JEFFREY REMEDIOS_* The goal for a Canadian major label was to find an interesting act, break them out in Canada, and then try to convince their international partners to release the record around the world. But it was absolutely impossible to get those records released anywhere else. If your band wasn't from the U.K. or the U.S., you were totally ignored, unless you were Céline Dion.

*DAVE BOOKMAN_* In conjunction with the mall-ternative explosion of Nirvana, you had Canadian major labels getting into the [indie-rock] business. But the infrastructure was lagging behind the music. You had a lot of the old guard trying to market a new product they didn't really understand, and they didn't understand that the people making the product had different values, a different sensibility, and that most of these bands couldn't really play [their instruments]. As soon as the major labels see that all these weird alternative bands can't play live and don't know how to do interviews, what do they do? Just like their classic-rock brethren before them, they went and signed pretty boys like Moist and Our Lady Peace — these fake alternative bands that were massively successful in Canada, but really no different than the hair bands of the '80s. They just had modern mall-ternative clothes.

*JOHN CROSSINGHAM_* You could liken the Canadian music scene to the progression of a glacier: there was an expansion in the early '90s and then it contracted, it receded, because all those indie labels either folded or just couldn't sustain that kind of popularity. Then the music scene went all rock radio and it just didn't feel the same: you went from talking about Treble Charger and Sloan and The Inbreds and Thrush Hermit to talking about Limblifter and Age of Electric. Even Treble Charger re-recorded "Red." And King Cobb Steelie, who were a huge influence on me, went to a major label and after that never really found their spot.

TORONTO WAS THE MAJOR-LABEL TOWN OF CANADA, AND SLOWLY EVERYONE REALIZED THAT [MODEL] WAS GOING NOWHERE, WHETHER IT WAS WITH TREBLE CHARGER OR hHEAD OR CHANGE OF HEART — THESE BANDS COULD ONLY REACH A CERTAIN POINT.

*JEFFREY REMEDIOS_* I started at Virgin Music Canada in 1997. That shop was built to sell pop music, not interesting art projects. It became harder and harder to take a risk. You had to worry about today, and worry about tomorrow morning on tomorrow morning. There was such a short-term life cycle that you ended up just chasing your tail around.

*JASON COLLETT_* The industry was in such turmoil. You'd get an A&R guy that was really into you and they'd have your demos and you'd feel ready to pen a deal. And then they lost their jobs because their company got bought out by another company. It was a really frustrating time. I think that the way Broken Social Scene tailspun out of that era was that guys like Andrew Whiteman and myself and Brendan Canning turned our backs on playing that game, because it was bullshit. The whole idea of going into the basement and playing with friends just for the joy of it was a big part of what happened later with Broken Social Scene.

YOU COULD LIKEN THE CANADIAN MUSIC SCENE TO THE PROGRESSION OF A GLACIER.

Jason Collett's band, Bird, featured at the Rivoli in Toronto, 1998. (JM)

Left to right: Danko Jones, Brendan Canning, and Kevin Drew, 1999. (BC)

WE
COLLIDE

BRENDAN CANNING MEETS LESLIE FEIST bHEAD ON

IF ANY ROCK BAND was poised to break out of Toronto in the mid-'90s, it was hHead. Fronted by Brendan Canning and Noah Mintz, the band both looked and sounded the part of Toronto's answer to Nirvana. Their debut release, *Fireman*, was a top seller in the indie section at HMV's flagship store and received ample attention from CFNY and MuchMusic. (Their first video, for "Flower," was directed by Mintz's high-school chum Hayden.) The band soon became the opening act for visiting alt-rock royalty like My Bloody Valentine and Dinosaur Jr., and they were one of the few local bands to sign directly with a prominent U.S. label: IRS, former benefactors of a young R.E.M. But the experience of touring their lukewarmly received 1995 release, *Jerk*, to small, disinterested crowds south of the border broke the band's spirit.

One of the only bright spots amid hHead's soul-crushing tour was an encounter with a young Calgary singer named Leslie Feist, whom Canning would later join in Toronto power-pop favourite By Divine Right (a union that coincided with a brief romantic relationship between the two). For Canning, the new band would rehash an old script: another major-label deal (this time with Sarah McLachlan's home base, Nettwerk Records), more marquee shows (a 1999 cross-Canada tour with The Tragically Hip), and little to show for it. By decade's end, Canning's career choices amounted to serving as a bassist-for-hire (Spookey Ruben, Blurtonia), an electronic-music producer (Cookie Duster), or a Top-40 footnote (having appeared on Len's 1999 hit single, "Steal My Sunshine"). He split the difference and became a DJ, spinning house music instead.

Like Canning, Feist left By Divine Right only to be faced with her own set of uncertainties. While she saved up her bar tips to record her first album, *Monarch*, her closest friends — aspiring electro-rap MCs Peaches and Chilly Gonzalez — had fled to Europe to forward their careers (a route also explored by Canning's roommate, Danko Jones). Meanwhile, Feist's new boyfriend, Toronto guitarist Andrew Whiteman, weathered a cycle of impoverishment and fortuitous windfalls that would earn him his new stage alias, the Apostle of Hustle. **United by their disillusionment, Canning, Feist, and Whiteman had formed a social scene — but without any breaks.**

Left to right: Jose Contreras, Leslie Feist, Mark Goldstein, and Brendan Canning of By Divine Right in Hamilton, Ontario, 1998. (SC)

Leslie Feist and By Divine Right in Hamilton, Ontario, 1998. (SC)

BRENDAN CANNING[1]_ When Noah and I started hHead, we wanted a deal within a year. We were just so naïve and didn't have a clue.

NOAH MINTZ_ hHead's first big show in Toronto was opening for My Bloody Valentine. Brendan landed those sorts of gigs by calling [promoter] Eliott Lefko incessantly. Brendan was the guy — if it was just me at the helm of hHead, it would've been a small band. Brendan was the one who had a clear idea of what he wanted. He works to get a show and makes sure things are arranged. That's a big part of his success, and why he's brought every band he's been in to the next level.

WE SIGNED A SHIT DEAL. IF WE WERE A BETTER BAND, WE COULD'VE SIGNED A BETTER DEAL, BECAUSE WE HAD INTEREST FOR SURE.

YVONNE MATSELL_ I've known Brendan forever. He used to call me when I was booking The Ultrasound and say, "I'm in a band called hHead — little h, capital H, e-a-d." It was a daily call from him — he used to drive us crazy!

ANDREW WHITEMAN_ I first met Canning when hHead played with The Bourbon Tabernacle Choir in '92. We were the first two bands at this huge Winnipeg rock festival that Pearl Jam flew in for in a helicopter. hHead had to go on at 11:00 a.m. and the Bourbons had to go on at noon. I remember smoking a doob in one of their hotel rooms and Canning lying on the bed with an acoustic guitar, just as he does now.

NOAH MINTZ_ At the time, the only serious deals we were entertaining were Warner Music Canada and IRS in the States. And then we did a show with 54-40, and they said, "Don't sign in Canada — you may not get any success outside of Canada, but at least you'll have a shot. If you sign in Canada, you'll be strung along for five to six years and have a half-

career in Canada." Canadian major labels at that time were signing Bootsauce and Rainbow Butt Monkeys, who turned into Finger Eleven — fucking garbage. So we went for the American record deal [with IRS] because we naïvely thought that touring the U.S. would get us the same support we got in Canada, which of course was not the case.

BRENDAN CANNING_ We signed a shit deal. If we were a better band, we could've signed a better deal, because we had interest for sure. But we could never pull off any of those big showcases; we didn't have the focus to play a good show during that time. We did six dates with The Tragically Hip, one month with the Goo Goo Dolls, a week and a half with that band Green Apple Quick Step. I remember thinking, "How the fuck are these guys on the radio?" And then you find out they had Pearl Jam's management. Those were bummer days.

DAVE BOOKMAN_ hHead broke my heart, because they really screwed up. They got $100,000 from [CFNY], they got a worldwide deal with IRS, and they made the worst record: *Jerk*. It shouldn't have been released. It showed none of the band's promise. I was so disappointed in that album and in myself, and I was left thinking that maybe this world isn't for us. Like, we can't win. Everyone becomes corrupt. If someone offered me $100,000, I'd probably screw around too.

NOAH MINTZ_ hHead did a big outdoor festival [InFest] in Calgary in 1994, and this band won an opening slot at this festival. It turned out to be Leslie Feist's band, Placebo. She was a really nice girl, and kinda looked freaky: she had braids and dreads and a nose ring, and she was a sixteen-year-old alternative girl. Brendan and I watched her set, and as soon as she started singing, we looked at each other like, "Holy shit!" We were blown away. That's when I gave her my phone number and said, "If you come

Brendan Canning browsing at Sonic Unyon record store, Hamilton, Ontario, 1998. (SC)

DINO SAFARI

warm up for the release of *Seven Year Itch*, a greatest-hits collection that hits stores Sept. 7 (it's the first Blonde release on CD). While a Toronto launch showcase will be invite-only, a full reunion tour is expected this fall. The **Northern Pikes** have also prepared a retrospective collection — the pride of Saskatoon will relive such hits as "Teenland" and "Girl With a Problem," along with some previously unreleased tracks, for this late October release.

While "Saturdays in Silesia" and "No More, No Less" still get regular rotation on Retro Nights the world over, **Rational Youth** have been penning new material in the classic new-wave vein. Founder

Tracey Howe has teamed with Toronto synth-pop devotees **Dave Rout** (INFOR/Mental) and **J.C. Cutz** (DIN) on a brand-new disc, *To the Goddess Electricity*. The trio has made a few live appearances in Toronto, and may sched-

[...] another Toronto singer **Sarah Slean** did just that at the first of three shows in support of her new CD, *Blue Parade*, at Ted's Wrecking Yard last Thursday. After being made to wait outside the club while Slean finished soundchecking and again inside, the crowd was buzzing louder than the overworked fan. Yet when Slean took the stage with a full band [...] **Swinghammer** and a string quartet, all was forgiven. During her quiet piano lul-

1994 road trip. The label should have hired a continuity person: two of the disc's tracks — **Meat Beat Manifesto**'s "She's Unreal" and **Type O Negative**'s "Haunted" — weren't released until 1996. Also, Toronto band **Alice** play the Horseshoe Aug. 23 in support of their new album *If You Only Knew*, available [...] entertainment, as erroneously reported here a few weeks back. ◄

Leslie Feist featured in *Eye Weekly*, 1999. (SB)

BY MICHAEL BARCLAY

Happy family values

Since moving from Calgary to Toronto several years ago, Leslie Feist has spent plenty of time playing the role of sideperson. But these days, the 23-year-old splits her time between two main gigs: rocking out as a guitarist in By Divine Right; and unleashing the quiet strength of her vocal cords on her own material, heard on her just-released debut CD, *Monarch*.

The common element in both projects is a celebratory sense of a musical event, which is an almost corny notion in an age when fans have seen and heard everything. The hushed intimacy of Feist's solo arrangements don't lend themselves as easily to the love-ins found at a BDR rockfest, yet they're two sides of the same coin.

LESLIE FEIST
with the Jim Guthrie Quintet, Tuesday, Aug. 24. The Rivoli, 332 Queen W. $5.

After delaying her solo career while BDR toured North America for the better part of a year, Feist is ecstatic to be finally performing material she recorded last summer. "It's unbelievable!" she enthuses. "I'm not downplaying how great it is to play with By Divine Right, but [playing solo shows] taps into more of me than [...] those BDR shows did."

Unlike most solo artists blessed with talent and charisma, Feist feels a bit self-conscious about hogging the spotlight. She spent her formative years in the Calgary punk band Placebo, which she recalls fondly as a communal experience akin to a surrogate family. "I was one-quarter of the songwriting, and everyone was equally committed," she says. "Then, getting into my own trip and being the sole source, I felt so sad, like 'Where's the community?' It's a different level of friendship, and I missed having that when I moved here."

Upon moving to Toronto, Feist quickly fell into the bass position in Noah's Arkweld, despite never really having played bass before. She also served time in Bodega, and prior to joining By Divine Right she had only played guitar to accompany her own songwriting. Innate skill and luck have written the rest of the story so far. When it came time to plant the seeds of her solo project, it was a [...]

suddenly be calling the shots.

"Musically, I didn't have to settle somewhere in the middle between four other people," she says. "It always ends up ambiguous when no one is getting what they want, like there's less strength in it. This is my project, but it's wicked to have all these creative, awesome people who are my buddies come and throw their two bits in. Then it felt larger than just me sitting in the basement with a four-track." (Feist's current band includes Kevin Fox, Dave Szigeti, Andrew Whiteman and Dean Stone.)

Monarch certainly sounds expansive, with Feist's confident, bell-clear vocals guiding the listener through engaging lyrics, jagged pop, beautiful ballads and, on several tracks, a string quartet. The string parts were arranged by Szigeti, whom Feist and the string quartet accompany in [...]

Leslie Feist steps out from the sidelines

[...] ments in his band, and they're just pop songs," she explains. "Having the quartet

turned into this possibility. So I challenged him one day [to arrange some songs], and the next day he had reams of paper with all these little black dots on them."

The lead-off track on *Monarch* features the chorus, "You know it's cool to love your family," sung with nary a trace of irony. Such a statement seems almost inherently uncool, and Feist admits that the song provokes odd reactions from people. "I've reached an age where I can see my family is really cool," she explains. "I'm 23, and any time up until you're about 21, within your family you're perceived as scrambling around without your shit together. My family's been so emotionally supportive through all this.

"I was searching around for lyrics, and I probably had a really nice conversation with my grandmother that day. When I brought it to a jam, I got red in the face and we were all laughing. Then I got a bit defensive about it," she says, laughing. "Some people are like, 'What the hell is with that?' When people love it, you know that they really love their family. Not to say that the people who think it's weird don't, but you're going to react from where you feel, and some people

to Toronto, call me." You knew this girl was going to be successful. The talent was just raw, pure.

LESLIE FEIST_ Placebo had won a city-wide high-school battle of the bands, and the prize was a slot at InFest. hHead played the spot right before us. My bass player was a huge hHead fan. In fact, she bought a Fender Jazzmaster because she heard the bass player from hHead, Brendan, used one. I remember Brendan had a long goatee, dyed some colour, and there was a lot of barefoot scissor-kicking. And then we hung out after the show and I became pen pals with Noah. I remember having my first sambuca in their van backstage.

NOAH MINTZ_ During hHead's last album [*Ozzy*, 1996], I just couldn't get into it. I needed a way to separate myself from the hHead thing. I felt the band was starting to plateau, and we had drummer problems. I needed to do something different, so Noah's Arkweld was purely a solo project. It spawned one song for a Squirtgun compilation, and then I got offered a bunch of shows from that.

LESLIE FEIST_ Noah and I had kept in touch, and then when Placebo first toured out east we played Dave Bookman's Nu-Music Nite at the Horseshoe. I was sitting at the merch table and these two guys came up all smiley, saying, "Hey, don't you recognize us?" Noah and Brendan had both grown the antecedents of the indie-rock beard. Dave Bookman said, "Why don't you come back and play next week if you're still in town?" So then Noah said, "If you're sticking around, I'm playing the first solo show of my life at the Rivoli," and it was part of Hayden's Hardwood Wednesdays night.

HAYDEN_ The idea of getting people who were in bands to play their songs acoustically was the whole impetus for Hardwood Wednesdays. It was really fun for Noah to hear his songs done that way.

LESLIE FEIST_ Noah said, "I want you to sing one of my songs." I had never sung anything quietly ever in my life, so that was major. I remember being backstage with the lyrics, the paper shaking in my hand — I wasn't going to be able to hide behind the noise. So I sang this weird song about abortion and bleeding. The chorus was, "I bleed, I bleed."

BRENDAN CANNING_ At the end of the hHead tour for *Jerk* I had started playing with Spookey Ruben, in 1995, and then at the end of *Ozzy* [hHead's final record] I started playing with By Divine Right. I was a bit lost . . . I started DJing. I did my first hit of ecstasy on November 28, 1996, and that was it. I thought, "Fuck, I love house music."

STEPHEN CHUNG_ Brendan was the DJ at every party I was going to. There was never a point hanging out with Brendan where he wasn't playing music. And he knew abso-fucking-lutely everybody in town. He couldn't walk down a street for a hundred yards without saying hi.

DANKO JONES_ Brendan and I lived together for almost four years. We were like The Odd Couple: he was Oscar, the lovable guy who was a little disorderly, and I was Felix, the neat, annoying stick-in-the-mud. He definitely knew a lot of people. The phone would ring off the hook for the whole day into the night. I quickly grew tired of the people who called for him. My phone manners weren't the best either. If you called our house, you had to make sure you didn't get the big prick on the phone. To this day I'm still apologizing to Brendan's friends for my phone etiquette.

LESLIE FEIST_ When I finally moved to Toronto [in 1996], I hadn't been in touch with Noah and Brendan in a year or two. I lost my voice, so I was going to come to Toronto, hang out, and see this

hHead poster, 1991. (BC)

BRENDAN, NOAH, ZAC, ROLAND

Peaches and Leslie Feist, 1999. (TCB)

doctor. And then I spent nine months in my dad's basement — I didn't know a soul. It didn't even dawn on me to contact those guys. I had been four-tracking tons in the basement and learning how to play guitar. And then my mom called from Calgary and said, "Hey, a guy from Toronto just called here looking for you." Noah had phoned 411 in Calgary looking for a Feist, and phoned my mom's house and said, "I'm looking for your daughter because I'm recording that song that she sang with me a year ago." So my mom gives me his number and I phone Noah, who happens to live a block from my dad's house! He said, "Pick keyboards or bass," so I played bass in Noah's Arkweld. I always say Noah's my ground zero — everyone I know right now in my life I can lead back to Noah. Even Chilly Gonzalez I met through Noah, because [future New Deal/Dragonette member] Dan Kurtz joined Noah's Arkweld and introduced me to Gonzo.

NOAH MINTZ_ When Leslie moved to Toronto, I wanted to get her in my band immediately. Noah's Arkweld led her to becoming friends with Brendan. Dan Kurtz from The New Deal was also in Noah's Arkweld at that time. Dan, who was in Que Vida with Andrew Whiteman at the time, went on to produce Leslie's first album [*Monarch*].

ANDREW WHITEMAN_ I had learned to four-track with Dave Wall from the Bourbons, and every year at Christmas we'd make an album together. We did it for six years, and one of our songs, "The Scene," ended up being a number one hit single in Canada for Gordie Johnson and Big Sugar. The song was originally called "Oh Wuh Oh Oh," and it was making fun of my new friends who I had met in the indie scene. It was a totally ironic, Pavement-style tune that Gordie, of course, stripped of all irony and turned into a number one song.

The royalties from "The Scene" basically kept me alive for a year. But I hustled, I did everything: I took care of kids, I was a bicycle courier, I worked as a PA for a women's TV station, I worked for a porn company. I probably should've retreated and gone into four-tracking, but I wanted to play live, so I hooked up with Dan Kurtz in Que Vida. Dan also started playing with Noah's Arkweld, and that's how I met Feist. I used to run around with Jose Contreras [of By Divine Right] a lot, and we went to We'ave, across the street from the AGO [Art Gallery of Ontario]. I remember we saw Feist play solo there. Jose and I walked into this room and stood stock-still. For those four minutes we looked at each other and said, "Holy fuck."

LESLIE FEIST_ I had started promoting a night at We'ave on Dundas called Ramrod Hurrah. It was like a cabaret; lineups would feature Peaches, Emily Haines, Jose Contreras, Gonzo — anyone who was around. I had been a huge fan of By Divine Right. *All Hail Discordia* was my number one album at that time. At the end of one night, Jose said, "I want you to come jam with us."

In that time I recorded *Monarch*, I was dating Whitey and living at 701 Queen West with Dave Szigeti. It was kind of a frat house — I don't know how many people already had keys cut when I moved in there. At one point I needed a roommate and I sort of knew Peaches through Gonzo but not super-well. She was going through a divorce and needed a place to live, so she moved in. It was amazing living with her. She was the hardest-working person I knew, teaching kids drama. That was part of Peaches's shows that I always loved; you could see the schoolteacher in her. She was always over-simplifying for the audience: "All right, everyone, now we're going to rock! Hands in the air!"

I would be hard-pressed to find another era of my life that rivals the potency and fertile ground of the 701. We were all on the same layer of the cultural sediment — meaning completely subterranean — and working all of our jobs. Everyone was in the same moneyless struggle. And somehow the clarity of knowing that my rent was $400 a month and I made $9 plus tips an hour was just super-clear: if I want that guitar, it's going to take me four months. Everyone was on the edge of many cliffs.

*ANDREW WHITEMAN_* Feist got into By Divine Right, which I thought was a disaster, because for me By Divine Right was always about being a trio. The last By Divine Right show I had seen before she joined was at the Reverb upstairs during Canadian Music Week, and Canning had just started playing bass for them. It was a hot show. I thought, "These guys are going to win!"

*LESLIE FEIST_* Canning was the twelfth person to join By Divine Right, and I was the thirteenth member — but I was the first time they added a fourth member. By Divine Right were signed to Nettwerk and went on tour with The Tragically Hip. But when you feel like an underdog, even if you're on a stage in front of 30,000 people, you're in on your own joke, like, "How did I end up here? This is fucking hysterical!" It was like a philosophical moving art installation: "I am totally invisible. I am up here, yet nobody's looking and nobody can see me because I'm a dot, and even if they are looking, nobody cares, because they're just waiting for the Hip to come on." I understood how big it looked from the outside and how inconsequential it was on the inside. I didn't want that to be a peak. I was twenty-two. We were making $250 a week with no per diems because it was all catered, and at the time I was like, "My rent's only $400, and I'm eating for free — okay!"

*ANDREW WHITEMAN_* My fears about By Divine Right were confirmed when they had gone on tour with the Hip for months and those guys were telling me, "We get our own practice room; we can jam before every show," and how great it was

opening for the Hip. Then they did two secret shows at the Rivoli, and I was like, "You fuckers have been practising?" They were way worse than I had ever heard them. I was mad because I thought Feist was diverting [from] her own [solo career], and I was mad at them because I was like, "Why bother? You don't need another guitarist."

*LESLIE FEIST_* What I didn't like was when the pressure Jose was feeling started changing the attitude toward why we were doing it. We were out for nine or ten months in 1999, and I remember we did a twenty-four-hour run home from Boulder, Colorado. When we dropped Goldy [drummer Mark Goldstein] off, I think he barely grunted goodbye. I got out and I don't even think I said goodbye. Nobody was speaking to each other. And it wasn't like we were all fighting; there was just this festering silence. Everyone had just battened down their hatches so hard to get home. Basically I never called Jose after that and he never called me.

*BRENDAN CANNING_* The last show we actually did together was that CBC show *Jonovision* — talk about anticlimactic. It was like, "We're done." Feist and I went through dating in the band, before she dated Whitey. We were getting paid shit. We had some good jams but we were never fully utilized. I had to be content to be the sideman. Bernard [Maiezza, from Change of Heart] had opened the shows on the By Divine Right/Change of Heart tour. He would play spacey keyboard stuff, and I said, "Maybe I can give you help arranging some of your beats." So at the end of By Divine Right, I started working more with Bernard on Cookie Duster.

*NOAH MINTZ_* Brendan was always playing with somebody, but his success was always sort of somebody else's success. I didn't think he was just the guy who played with everybody but never did anything on his own. He's an amazing songwriter.

BRENDAN CANNING_ I had played on four songs with Len [on 1996's *Get Your Legs Broke*], and I had my turntables set up at [Len frontman] Mark Costanzo's place and was helping on another tune, "Steal My Sunshine." Mark didn't really need me musically; he also had Buck 65 and Sixtoo, so he was probably like, "I'm not going to be dying to keep this guy around." But Mark got me some money [for "Steal My Sunshine"] — he got me $3,000. I got the cheque, went to Songbird, and bought the Boomerang pedal and a bass micro-synth. The Boomerang became my go-to pedal in Broken Social Scene — it's like a poor man's sampler.

LESLIE FEIST_ Gonzales was signed to Warner Music Canada when I met him; he had just made his second album, *Wolfstein*, and Warner wanted to shelve it. But it was the record where he caught a whiff of what matters to him. He felt the music he was making wasn't fitting in here. He had a French passport, so Peaches and Gonzo went on a two-month-long European trip and they literally back-packed through Europe. But in their backpack, Gonzo had a CDJ [turntable-styled CD player] and a couple of CD folders with Dionne Warwick, Burt Bacharach, Kraftwerk — all this amazing, different stuff — and Peaches had the MC505 Groovebox, and I don't think at that point she had made a beat yet. They'd arrive in a city, look for some hipsters, and say, "Hey, what's a really cool bar you guys hang out at?" They'd go there and play in the corner — these three-hour noise sculptures, free-form stuff. It had nothing to do with what either of them would go on to do, but when they played in Berlin, they played the Kitty-Yo bar — they didn't know Kitty-Yo was also a label. This guy Raik Hölzel basically signs Gonzo on the spot. So Gonzo moved to Berlin because a window opened for him there.

DANKO JONES_ We turned our backs on Canada because there wasn't really any place to play, and the places that were there just led to nowhere. So our options were break up and get full-time jobs or keep going. Luckily an avenue opened for us in Europe. There was a label [Sweden's Bad Taste Records] that wanted to sign us and we just grabbed it.

BRENDAN CANNING[2]_ hHead, Len, Spookey Ruben, and By Divine Right — I was a part of all those [Canadian music industry] infrastructures at one time or another and playing the game of "Oh, this guy's interested and that guy's interested . . ." By the end, it really made me nauseous.

INTRO TO THE PRESSURE KIDZ

HOW THE ESA
MADE THE BSS

IT'S A CLICHÉ that rock bands form at art schools, but even if he didn't attend the Etobicoke School of the Arts — a multidisciplinary alternative high school in Toronto's solidly middle-class westernmost borough — Kevin Drew would undoubtedly be in a band. As old friends (Joris Jarsky, Eric Yealland) and future bandmates (Emily Haines, Amy Millan) tell it, the teenaged Kevin Drew had already assumed the charismatic qualities of a bandleader well before he knew how to play guitar. And the array of music he was absorbing at the time — the discordant indie-rock of Sonic Youth and Dinosaur Jr., the heart-on-sleeve/lump-in-throat expressionism of Jeff Buckley, the atmospheric film scores of Ennio Morricone, the ambient soundscapes of Brian Eno, the jazz/dub-reggae–inspired post-rock of Tortoise and the Dirty Three — would all prove to be crucial components of Broken Social Scene's musical alchemy.

But if the ESA has come to be known as Broken Social Scene's ground zero, then ground one would be Oakwood Collegiate Institute, which counted James Shaw, Evan Cranley, and future Stars co-founders Torquil Campbell and Chris Seligman among its student body. The union of these two circles — facilitated by Haines and Shaw's budding romance — would eventually carry these friends from high-school halls to concert halls. But it would be a few years before they all realized the benefits of strength in numbers: upon graduation, they would each go their separate ways and try their individual luck in the Canadian music-industry crapshoot.

KEVIN DREW_ Things can form you at an early age, and the ESA definitely did that to me. It set the tone of what kind of human being I was going to be, and how I went about feeling friendship — being addicted to that connection.

EMILY HAINES_ Kevin actually grew up in Etobicoke, but the rest of [their friends at ESA] were all misfits from shitty towns who came to that school because there were no jocks. You would have punk-rock kids — who would normally get beaten up by jocks — totally getting along with skateboarders. All those rules of high school were erased at the ESA.

EMILY AND I STARTED SINGING TOGETHER IN HIGH SCHOOL, AND WE HAD A BAND CALLED EDITH'S MISSION. KEVIN WAS ACTUALLY OUR MANAGER FOR A WEEK.

AMY MILLAN_ I started at the Etobicoke School of the Arts in grade eleven. On the first day of school, I got lost looking for the music class. This girl came up to me and said, "Are you looking for the music class?" I said, "Yeah." She said, "Me too. Are you new?" "Yeah." "Me too." And that was Emily Haines. I lived in Cabbagetown [on the east side of downtown Toronto] and Emily was living with her sister [nearby] at Sherbourne. We lived five blocks from each other, so a quick friendship formed.

JORIS JARSKY_ When we went to the Etobicoke School of the Arts, we had Kevin Drew, Emily Haines, Amy Millan, Andre Ethier from The Deadly Snakes, Josh Reichmann from Tangiers, author Ibi Kaslik, and Micah Meisner, a five-time MuchMusic Video Award–winning director. There was definitely a core group of people who have gone on and worked within the arts. Kevin, Amy, and Emily were all drama majors . . . which they still are now. They just call themselves musicians.

KEVIN DREW_ Everybody in this crew had past relations in some way, whether it was two degrees of separation or full-on heart attacks. This band had drama attached to it from the beginning. But what most people call drama, I call reality. I've always said that the [high-school] hallway sets the rules for life.

JORIS JARSKY_ Kevin was the most popular person in school in grade nine. He had an adoring group of older women that he used hang out with, like Ibi, Amy, and Emily.

AMY MILLAN_ Emily and I started singing together in high school, and we had a band called Edith's Mission. Kevin was actually our manager for a week. We had this crazy show at the Horseshoe and it was totally sold out and Kevin said, "That's it. I'm your manager." But then we kind of fell apart and Emily went off to do other stuff.

EMILY HAINES_ Kevin was fascinated by the tight-knit friendships of girls. Objectively speaking, when you look at it, everybody [in this circle of friends] has fucked everybody, and to me it's not that sinister — it was really innocent and lovely. But the friendships become so intense we all needed to get away from each other [after graduation]. And then we realized that, for whatever reason, we were never going to get away from each other.

JORIS JARSKY_ Kevin was always rocking the plaid shirt. He was Mr. indie-rock non-stop all the time. He was always interested in music, but I have to say, when his brother Cam gave him a guitar when he was nineteen, I remember thinking, "What the fuck is he going to do with that?" Whether or not he could play the guitar or piano is debatable, but he could always write a song.

KEVIN DREW_ I was the Sonic Youth/Dinosaur Jr./My Bloody Valentine kid — those were my mainstream bands. But on the other side, I was into classical music. I had mononucleosis in grade eight;

Amy Millan and Emily Haines (*top and bottom right*), 1996. (JM)

Amy Millan and Emily Haines performing at the Horseshoe Tavern with Edith's Mission, 1996. (JM)

it was Earth Day and I happened to be watching MuchMusic and they showed the Ennio Morricone video from *The Mission* soundtrack. That just set me off on the instrumental loop that introduced me to Brian Eno, Steve Reich, and all kinds of crazy bands like the Cranes.

ERIC YEALLAND_ I met Kevin in 1994. He was selling sunglasses in Preloved on Queen Street. He was eighteen, and was the worst sunglasses sales-man of all time. He would just chat up the girls in the store. He was a charm-ing young guy. I took him to see Jeff Buckley at the Danforth Music Hall. Music was the thing that brought us together. And there was something that made me feel very big-brotherly toward him.

KEVIN AND I WERE TOO ROMANTIC TO ACTUALLY BE IN A REAL RELATION-SHIP. WE HAD A MUTUAL MUSE KIND OF VIBE, AND I THINK WE KNEW THAT THEN.

KEVIN DREW_ I had been with Emily, and after I had fallen out with her, she started up with Jimmy Shaw. And he was just so amazing to me from the beginning. It was just such a wicked ex-girlfriend's-boyfriend situa-tion, though Emily and I weren't exes by nature; we were just teenagers having a modern romance — it was all about that movie kiss.

JAMES SHAW_ I met Emily in July of '97. We were at the Horseshoe watching a really bad white funk band, and Emily came up to me and said, "This is the most abysmal shit I've ever seen," and I said, "I totally agree . . . Wanna go out?" And that was that. I had one of those rehearsal spaces on Richmond Street, and two weeks later we were hav-ing a party there and Kevin showed up. He and Emily got into this huge fight right away. I remem-ber he came up to me and said, "I'm really sorry," and I was like, "That's totally cool — just go fight it out until you're all done, and then come back in and we'll hang out."

KEVIN DREW_ Jimmy was just making sure we figured it out. He was like, "I really want you guys to settle this." He had this idea of "You settle this, and it's better for everybody." And I loved him for that. It's the reason I consider him my husband to this day.

EMILY HAINES_ Jimmy saved my friendship with Kevin. Kevin and I were too romantic to actually be in a real relationship. We had a mutual muse kind of vibe, and I think we knew that then. If we had ever gotten close enough to really be in a relationship, it would've been horrible. I remember having a con-versation with him at his parents' swimming pool. We agreed that we were meant to put [their rela-tionship] into music. It was like a blood pact.

AMY MILLAN_ I didn't think Kevin liked me very much when we were at the ESA together, but then when I was at Concordia [University in Montreal], we reacquainted ourselves. He used to come to Montreal a lot because his brother Cam was living there, and Kevin had become friends again with Emily, who had also moved there. She had a get-together at her house and Kevin was there and we became friends again. I remember recording with Kevin in '96 in his basement on his four-track — if we were together, we were going to be playing music. That's what we did for recreation.

EMILY HAINES_ Jimmy had just come back from Julliard and I had just come back from Montreal to Toronto for the summer when we met. All that was happening musically in Toronto back then was bad funk. Meanwhile, there was all this amazing music happening on the street level, but the major labels were immune to it. I call it "the acid-wash phenom-enon" — all the major-label people in their acid-wash jeans and leather jackets were pandering to American major labels and had no interest in what was actually happening [in Toronto].

Kevin Drew, 1995. (EH)

Chris Seligman of Stars and James Shaw of Metric, 1998. (EH)

James Shaw and Emily Haines of Metric, 1998. (EH)

*EVAN CRANLEY_* When I was eighteen, I played trombone with Gypsy Soul and we had a deal with A&M Records. We had some medium MuchMusic rotation on a single called "Black Book Man." We sold about 15,000 records, which was fine. Didn't see a penny of it. To this day I'm convinced I got fucked over for money. The singer left and then we got a new singer, and it was very uninspiring. After I left that band, I got called up to do an audition for Colin James's Little Big Band, and I didn't get that. I always kind of shunned the brass player's career choices — I didn't want to end up in the orchestra pit playing *Cats* for three years eight times a week.

Then I was playing a lot with Mambo Urbano and backed up Jerry Gonzalez a couple of times playing salsa music. I had a residency at Lava Lounge on Wednesday nights. Mambo Urbano ended up headlining the Montreal Jazz Festival, which was great. [Toronto swing-band leader] Big Rude Jake phoned up after and I toured two years straight with him. I wore the zoot suit, and me and the trumpet player choreographed dance moves. It was a thrill playing with him because he was really the first boss I ever had — he cracked the whip pretty hard if you stepped out of line musically. I was pretty young: twenty-two, twenty-three. Jake took me around the world — that was really fun. The horn was a good way of making a living because no one was playing trombone.

*AMY MILLAN_* When I moved back to Toronto, I had my band 16 Tons. We played all my own songs, but I just wanted to play in a band so badly that I was like, "I'll share all the songwriting credits; we'll do this together!" I was planning to move to New York to do other things, but then I met this manager — Patrick Sandbrook, who was managing Sarah Harmer — and he said to me, "I want to represent you." The offer kind of fell into my lap, so I started playing big shows quite early. My first concert was at the Stardust Picnic, opening for Blue Rodeo. It's funny, Chris Seligman and Evan Cranley were postering for that show; that's how they were making their money at the time. They got paid ten bucks an hour to do it and Evan got a free pass to that show, and I saw him there.

*JAMES SHAW_* In the fall of '98, Emily and I got this little rehearsal space on Mercer Street, and that's when we did our first real collaboration. We were called Mainstream. It was a couple more years before we called ourselves Metric. We went to New York in June '98, and I was running this crazy loft — eight bedrooms, 5,000 square feet. We had shows there. Nick [Zinner] from the Yeah Yeah Yeahs lived there; years later Karen [Orzelek of the Yeah Yeah Yeahs] moved in and a bunch of guys from TV on the Radio and Liars moved in. But in the early days it was a full-on ghetto; like nobody had money to buy a bun. It was fun because I was twenty-three. I never partied back then — anytime that I wasn't in a restaurant working, I was at home making music.

*KEVIN DREW_* Grunge had come, blown up, and died. But then 1994 through '98 were the greatest fucking years to buy records. Suddenly you had Tortoise, Sea and Cake, and Dirty Three, and then Low and then the Mo' Wax Records stuff. That was who I turned to for the modern ideal of the sounds I wanted.

STOMACH SONGS

K.C. ACCIDENTAL
GOES FOR THE GUT

IF BROKEN SOCIAL SCENE was born of a creative marriage between Kevin Drew and Brendan Canning, then Charles Spearin was Drew's first steady relationship. As classmates at Toronto music-industry training school the Harris Institute — where local club booker Yvonne Matsell served as an instructor — the two bonded over a love of abstract instrumental indie-rock bands like Tortoise and Montreal's Godspeed You! Black Emperor, both of which spurred on Drew's burgeoning interest in soundtrack music.

Spearin was the bassist for the Toronto experimental-rock ensemble Do Make Say Think, whose guitarist, Ohad Benchetrit, was another Harris alum. The band's celebrated 1998 self-titled debut — picked up for international release by Godspeed's Constellation Records label — provided the tonic for Toronto's post-grunge hangover: lengthy instrumental movements that drew equally from dub reggae's emphasis on subsonic rhythms and panoramic production and psychedelic rock's penchant for blissful noise and euphoric release.

Spearin and Drew formed K.C. Accidental in 1998, around the same time Drew entered another partnership, with his future wife, Jo-Ann Goldsmith. K.C. Accidental's intimate instrumentals served as the come-down to Do Make Say Think's epic surges. True to the project's humble origins and aspirations, its first album, *Captured Anthems for an Empty Bathtub*, was housed in handmade packaging and sold exclusively through Queen Street indie-music mecca Rotate This. But in what would become a familiar pattern for Drew, the team of two soon expanded to include a random assortment of friends — drummer Justin Peroff, Big

Rude Jake trombonist/future Stars member Evan Cranley, Treble Charger guitarist Bill Priddle, Metric's James Shaw and Emily Haines, journeyman singer/songwriter Jason Collett — who all shared a desire to explore musical territory beyond standard pop-song structure.

The newly fortified group played a handful of shows at the (now defunct) King Street lounge The Mockingbird and released their second album, *Anthems for the Could've Bin Pills*, in 2000 on Toronto ambient-electronica specialty label Noise Factory Records (run by Joe English, whom Drew had first met through a Harris school project). While the album received enthusiastic reviews in the local weeklies and earned them gigs in Montreal, K.C. Accidental remained a modest word-of-mouth curio. But their sweetly swelling compositions struck a chord with someone who had all but turned his back on indie-rock music: Brendan Canning.

Charles Spearin and Kevin Drew, 1998. (KD)

Kevin Drew, somewhere in Europe while on tour with Do Make Say Think, 2000. (KD)

Charles Spearin recording the first K.C. Accidental album in Kevin Drew's bedroom, 1998. (KD)

YVONNE MATSELL_ I was teaching band-booking at the Harris Institute and Kevin Drew was in my class, and he was just a charming, irritating bastard. I really loved him — he stood out from the crowd.

KEVIN DREW_ I went to Harris for production and I took four courses, and quite early on I realized, "I'm fucked. This is all mathematics." So I decided to go into the management side, not the production side.

JOE ENGLISH_ In 1997 [his label] Noise Factory was working with [the band] Nancy Despot. They were different in the way they were bringing the "big show" back. A lot of people pigeonholed them as glam rock, but they weren't a glam band, they were just entertaining. That was something that was lacking in the whole grunge movement — it was anti any kind of rock-star idea. Kevin Drew was going to school at Harris, and one of his school projects was to manage a band, and that's how I met Kevin. He was a fan of Nancy Despot. He was kind of quiet at the time, a little bit more reserved, but he was always very positive and always wanting to do something to help out. But then [Nancy Despot's lead singer] Brian [Gundstone] died. I didn't really know what to do with the label after that.

CHARLES SPEARIN_ I met Kevin Drew at the Harris Institute for the Arts. He came up to me outside and said, "You look like a guy who likes Tortoise." And that was kind of it. Tortoise was the icebreaker.

JO-ANN GOLDSMITH_ When I met Kevin, he had just dropped out of Harris. He was twenty years old and he had just moved out of his mother's house — which isn't really that attractive for someone like me who was five years older and had their shit

together. But he's charming and has so much charisma. Even then he had a highly developed sense of self-esteem, and he knew exactly what he wanted.

YVONNE MATSELL_ Kevin knew he was going to be somebody. I bumped into him after he finished school and asked, "What are you doing?" He said he was working in the studio — he wanted to compose film scores.

KEVIN DREW_ I always say everything [in contemporary Canadian indie-rock] started with Godspeed You! Black Emperor and Constellation Records — that was the crack, the icebreaker that allowed [Canadian indie] bands to get recognized in places that just seemed so foreign and unattainable, like Stockholm or Tokyo, when you were just trying to get to Vancouver or New York.

JOHN CROSSINGHAM_ Godspeed You! Black Emperor was the next big moment in Canadian indie music. They came from Montreal, they didn't sound like anyone else, and everyone around the world was going apeshit for them. They had everything: great music, integrity, mystique, an independent label — Constellation Records — that was entirely behind it and that had its own catalogue that was in the process of becoming better and better. That was the first time I could remember when people around the world were looking at Canada and not joking or saying, "Here comes another Canadian band that sounds like another popular American or British band."

OHAD BENCHETRIT_ Do Make Say Think started about twelve years ago [in 1995]. The whole idea was to make music and to have fun. I don't think I realized there was commercial potential until I saw Godspeed You! Black Emperor break through. I thought, "Oh my god, this music has nothing to do with the kind of music major labels are looking

Kevin Drew and Evan Cranley, 2000. (LF)

K.C. Accidental set list, 1998. (KD)

for." Back then, Canadian music was Bryan Adams. Canadian music was shit. Canadian music was something we had to excuse. It wasn't until Godspeed that we felt we could honestly make the kind of music we wanted to make — for the sake of making music — and actually have it go further than your community, have it take you to places like Europe and maybe even Japan or Australia. Watching a Canadian band get to Europe and get success both critically and commercially, and seeing the eyes of the music press were now turned toward Canada instead of Canadians turning outward . . . that gave everybody a bump, like our music was legit and we could actually see this through.

I THOUGHT, "I CAN'T BELIEVE SOMEONE IN TORONTO IS MAKING THIS MUSIC — IT'S SO FUCKING GREAT."

JOHN CROSSINGHAM_ I drew a lot of strength from Do Make Say Think, who were also on Constellation and making some really great stuff. I thought, "I can't believe someone in Toronto is making this music — it's so fucking great."

KEVIN DREW_ I wanted to start this band Djula with Charles and this gentleman Stephen Crowhurst and my friend Derek Stevens. And then I called James Shaw, because I had met him through Emily and knew he played trumpet.

JAMES SHAW_ Everything was still juvenile back then — it was really rudimentary instrumental music. Kevin was listening to all these downbeat instrumental records like Tortoise. Djula was an attempt for Kevin and Charlie to start doing what they were listening to.

CHARLES SPEARIN_ Djula did two shows at the Mockingbird — one with Do Make Say Think, which was Kevin's first show as a band. I had done one show with Kevin at Holy Joe's opening for Amy Millan, just improvising. I think Kevin just decided he wanted to make music with me. So Derek said, "Just go make music with Charlie." The first recording of K.C. Accidental we did was in Kevin's parents' basement.

JUSTIN PEROFF_ I was working at HMV and I quit because I got an acting gig. I auditioned for this show *Straight Up*, and I got the part — I was Sarah Polley's boyfriend on the show. Marc Cohen, who played my best friend, said, "You have to meet my friend Kevin Drew — I know you guys would get along and I know you will probably end up making music together." I didn't drive at the time, and I'm terrible with directions, so I told them to take 16th Avenue all the way to my parents' place in Markham. The car ride took forever, and if anybody knows Kevin's patience with these sorts of things, he wasn't very happy. He didn't even want to come in the house to meet my folks. So I sit down in the car, introduce myself, and he's very aloof. But we talked a bit and cracked some jokes. I was the Sonic Youth fan and he was the absolute Dinosaur Jr. fan — it was almost competitive in a playful way.

CHARLES SPEARIN_ Kevin wanted to call K.C. Accidental "Thomas Birchcroft," because Thomas is his middle name and Birchcroft is the street he grew up on, so it's like his porn-star name. I didn't like it. There was a lot of hemming and hawing and then he came up with K.C. Accidental, based on our initials. I liked the "Accidental" part because it encourages the unexpected, which is what we were going for at the time. And in jazz-nerd talk, an accidental is a note that's outside of a scale — he didn't know that, but I did.

JUSTIN PEROFF_ I was at The Mockingbird on a date, and Kevin came in with the orange construction-paper K.C. Accidental record and he put it on, and

SAMSTAG

20.
11.
'99

DO
MAKE
SAY
THINK

(CAN)

REITSCHULE

AB

Poster for a Do Make Say Think show in Belgium, November 20, 1999. (CS)

Left to right: Justin Peroff, Pauli the soundman, Kevin Drew, and Justin Small playing road hockey at the Ferry Docks in Dover, England, 2000. (CS)

Left to right: James Payment, Charles Spearin, Ohad Benchetrit, Dave Mitchell, and Justin Small of Do Make Say Think, 1999. (AD)

I was like, "This is really beautiful music — I can't believe this is coming out of Toronto." And then he said to me, "We will definitely be making music together." When it came to the release party for this CD, he called me up to be the drummer, and through practising songs on that record, we ended up writing new songs for the following K.C. Accidental record.

JOE ENGLISH_ There was just a pure emotional buildup in all the K.C. songs. The songs are what Kevin says they are: it's stomach music, it hits you right in the gut. It's hard to avoid that when you listen to it. And it kind of blew me away. I was like, "This is Kevin doing this?" I had known Kevin as a gadabout kind of guy who likes to talk, but I had no idea he was a creative force.

OHAD BENCHETRIT_ I don't think Kevin would disagree with the fact that, at that time — I wouldn't say he was infatuated with the Do Makes but, like anybody, when you come across something you really like and you're inspired by it, it's hard not to imitate in a certain way. You're drawing inspiration, ideas, and that's where the similarity happens. And you can't fault him for that, because the Do Makes have been just as guilty with other bands — imitation is the sincerest form of flattery. But Kevin's a smart guy. Instead of just ripping something off, he'll actually grab the people that do it. So if K.C. Accidental sounded like the Do Makes — well, fuck, one of the two members is in the Do Makes!

KEVIN DREW_ The first K.C. Accidental record was only available in one store: there were a hundred of them in Rotate This. And the album went number one there. I still have the chart. It was us, then Tortoise's *TNT*, then Dirty Three's *Ocean Songs*. Those guys [at Rotate This] started it all for us. They were essential.

JUSTIN PEROFF_ There was no plan to K.C. Accidental. We were just friends playing music together and really enjoying it. It wasn't rock music, it was just beautiful. I remember the first time playing with a horn section, and there were these instrumental breaks that could go in any direction. There was a lot of trust. The first K.C. performance [at The Mockingbird], Emily Haines opened up the show. Jimmy Shaw was in the K.C. band, Justin Small [from Do Make Say Think] made an appearance, Charles Spearin, of course, Kevin Drew, myself, and Evan Cranley playing trombone. There really weren't a lot of people at that show, but there was a huge rainstorm afterward — and if you ask anybody about that night, they'll talk about the rainstorm. I don't want to be a hippy-dippy guy, but there was definitely something special about that night.

EMILY HAINES_ I have one of the most amazing memories of that Mockingbird show. There was an unbelievable rainstorm, and I remember standing with everyone, thinking, "This is really an amazing group of people." Around that time we recorded "Them (Pop Song #3333)" in his parents' basement, and we recorded "Backyards" at Harris.

JASON COLLETT_ Kevin was a fan; he had seen me play a couple years before and he came up and talked to me, and I would bump into him around town. I played on some K.C. Accidental stuff he and Charlie were working on.

BILL PRIDDLE_ My wife at the time was a book publicist, and she worked for [Kevin's father] David Drew, and Kevin was also working for him at the time. And, in her words, Kevin said, "Your boy's in Treble Charger!" Kevin and I met, and very shortly afterward he said, "Come to the studio and play on my record," which was the second K.C. Accidental record. They were doing it in the CIUT basement studios. I came over at midnight and he and Charles

Wednesday September 10th at Holy Joes
* * *
Lenni Jabour
Amy Millan
Kevin Drew
and guests @ 9:30 ♪

Do Make Say Think's 1998 self-titled debut album on Constellation Records. (CR)

Flyer for a show at Holy Joe's in Toronto, featuring Amy Millan and Kevin Drew, 1999. (JM)

Holy Joes is located at Queen+Bathurst: SOUTH EAST CORNE

anthems for the could've bin pills
k.c. accidental

K.C. Accidental's 2000 album, *Anthems for the Could've Bin Pills*, on Noise Factory Records. (NFR)

were there, and I swear, even though Charles is the sweetest guy, he gave me a look like, "This was not my idea." I did one distorted guitar take and Kevin said, "Okay, I don't think that's quite it. . . ." So I said, "Can we listen to it? There might be some stuff there." And he said, "You know, the song's seventeen minutes long and there's really no playback — you just do it and you move on."

EVAN CRANLEY_ Kevin reached out to me — I just remember going over into that studio at CIUT with Justin and being totally into the music. It was a different approach to music, and I had never done that instrumental ethereal stuff. That's what I loved about doing music with Kevin: I could take brass instruments and just apply them to different kinds of music. Kevin doesn't really approach music-making as a musician. He's more like a movie director in the way that he talks about what he wants to happen. This beautiful accident seems to happen when he gets involved. I knew right away from those sessions that I'd be making music with him for a long time.

JOE ENGLISH_ There was a lot of financial and emotional investment in Nancy Despot, and that started to take its toll on me. But, starting around 2000, I decided to put it all in the past and start Noise Factory anew again. I started chatting with Kevin, who helped me put together the *Beautiful Noise* compilation. It was based on my own personal musical history, which was based a lot in electronic, experimental music, and radio shows like [CBC's] *Brave New Waves*. I was also in a reflective mood at the time and was listening to new stuff coming out of Warp Records. When Kevin did the first K.C. Accidental album, I don't think he even considered bringing it to me. I guess he thought my musical influences weren't his. But when we got together to talk about the compilation and he gave me a track, I fell in love with the band and

pursued them, because he told me he was working on a second album.

BRENDAN CANNING_ My friend Richie Curetan had told me to check out K.C. Accidental. I'd see Kev around town every now and then, and he had given me a flyer to go see his band play at The Mockingbird. He was always a likable guy and a friendly face.

KEVIN DREW_ I first met Canning [in 1999] because I saw Feist on the television set [in the video for By Divine Right's "Come for a Ride"] and said, "Who the fuck is that?" I remember being at the 606 on King Street and seeing Canning and Leslie making out in the hallway, and I thought, "There's that 'Come for a Ride' girl!" I happened to meet Brendan after [that relationship] was over.

KEVIN DOESN'T REALLY APPROACH MUSIC-MAKING AS A MUSICIAN. HE'S MORE LIKE A MOVIE DIRECTOR IN THE WAY THAT HE TALKS ABOUT WHAT HE WANTS TO HAPPEN.

BRENDAN CANNING_ This one night, me, Richie, and Stephen Chung were sitting at Fruition on College Street, and Kevin had the new K.C. record, so he went off with Chung to go listen to it. Me and Richie went back to his place to smoke a joint, and I said, "What about that guy Kevin Drew?" Richie played the first K.C. record and I just sort of said absently, "Maybe I'll make this kid a star." We had this one night where me and Kev and Richie and Spookey Ruben all went out together and got wasted at the Clear Spot. That's how it all started.

I BELIEVE IN THE GOOD LIFE

THREE GUT RECORDS, WAVELENGTH, THE HIDDEN CAMERAS, AND RADIO MONDAYS DO THEIR COMMUNITY SERVICE

THE DYING DAYS of 1999 were a great time for computer programmers and media pundits plugging their Y2K-bug books, but they were particularly depressing for independent Toronto musicians looking to play for people other than friends or family. The same major-label A&R reps who only a few years earlier were seeking out innovative rock acts like Change of Heart and King Cobb Steelie were now being directed to sign teenybopper pop (Sky), ersatz swing (the Johnny Favourite Swing Orchestra), or glossed-over grunge (Nickelback).

The knee-jerk response to this sorry state of affairs was to get out of town. Evan Cranley and Amy Millan joined their old friends Torquil Campbell and Chris Seligman in New York to form their electro-pop outfit Stars. Emily Haines and James Shaw had relocated their new band, Metric, from Toronto to New York to London and then back to New York to pursue (ultimately fruitless) label and publishing opportunities. After recording her solo debut, *Monarch*, Feist eventually chose to tour Europe with her friend Peaches instead of promoting her own album back home.

But in the wake of this exile from Queen Street, the new millennium marked a new beginning for Toronto indie-music culture. Soundscapes — a CD store that positioned itself as a more upscale cousin to Queen Street's Rotate This — introduced esoteric music to the more upwardly mobile College Street crowd and became a hub for local musicians (some of whom, like Raising the Fawn front man John Crossingham, actually worked there). Across the street at Ted's Wrecking Yard, three long-time indie-scene mainstays — Jonathan Bunce, Duncan

MacDonnell, and Derek Westerholm — launched Wavelength, a weekly indie-music showcase (and accompanying zine) whose mission was to unite Toronto's isolated musical niches and create a greater whole. **(In December 2000, Kevin Drew would perform a solo set at Wavelength under the name John Tesh Jr. and the Broken Social Scene — the first-ever public appearance of the BSS banner.) In a similar spirit, Jason Collett introduced Radio Mondays, a weekly songwriters' workshop at Rancho Relaxo that brought musicians of diverse backgrounds together to preview or, if the mood struck, improvise on works-in-progress.**

The community was also reinvigorated by some domestic imports. Guelph residents Lisa Moran and Tyler Burke moved their upstart Three Gut Records label to Toronto, bringing boldly unconventional promotional strategies and a stable of endearingly off-kilter artists, including Gentleman Reg, Jim Guthrie, and Royal City, the last of which temporarily featured Feist. This roster would soon include soul-punk prodigal sons Constantines, a Guelph-bred quartet powered by the intense call-and-response interaction between guitarist/vocalists Bry Webb and Steve Lambke. And from Toronto satellite city Mississauga, Joel Gibb's Hidden Cameras both challenged and redefined prevailing indie-rock orthodoxies. They packed the stage with virtuoso musicians and amateur artists alike, booked performances in atypical venues from churches to porno theatres, and transformed each concert into a ramshackle spectacle that incorporated homemade murals, projected lyric sheets (to encourage singalongs), cheerleading crowd-participation exercises, and explicit lyrical and visual references to gay sex.

To be a fan no longer meant just showing up and buying a T-shirt — in the Cameras' case, it was more about getting onstage and taking it off. If the end of the twentieth century brought the end of anything, it was that of the crossed-arms cynic standing at the back of the club passing silent judgement.

Top and bottom: The crowd at the Three Gut Records launch, 1999. (TCB)

Tyler Clark Burke and Leslie Feist's Envelope Project, 1999. (TCB)

Leslie Feist and Royal City, 2000. (TCB)

*EVAN CRANLEY_* The Canadian music industry in 1998–99 was abysmal; it didn't nurture musicians or talent in any way. And that's why people left. There was amazing pop music happening in New York, and I went down there in December 1999 and joined Stars. I was constantly back and forth between doing tours with Big Rude Jake, hanging out in New York with Stars, and then taking trains back to Toronto to work with what was to become Broken Social Scene.

*AMY MILLAN_* I kind of had a meltdown and ran away to L.A. for a little while. But L.A. is such a shithole, so I couldn't really handle it, and I really missed having dinner with people who would actually look you in the eye instead of over your shoulder, waiting for somebody famous to walk into the room. So I came back to Toronto and then I got a call from Stars. That was in December 1999.

*JAMES SHAW_* Metric were chasing a bunch of deals. Emily and I ended up doing this demo deal with Warner Brothers in '99. We knew they wouldn't pick [their music] up [for release], because it wasn't right for them. But then some dude in England called us up and said, "I'm starting a management company, and I think you guys are great. You should move here . . . I'll fund you guys." So we went to the U.K. at the beginning of 2000 and we got a publishing deal right away with Chrysalis. We did another demo deal with Independiente; we flew back to New York, did a week in Stephen Hague's studio in Woodstock, which resulted in terrible music, and I just didn't know enough back then to second-guess what people were telling me. We went with this flow of overly fed expense-account A&R people who really didn't give a shit. By the end of the year, we decided we wanted to get the hell out of England and get back to New York.

*EMILY HAINES_* When we came back from England after two years of writing demos for record labels and recording [Metric's debut album] *Grow Up and Blow Away*, we decided, "We're going to be a fucking live band." Having that loft in New York was a big influence on us, with Liars and Yeah Yeah Yeahs and TV on the Radio all living there. We just thought, "Fuck recording, fuck record labels, fuck everything. We're just going to be a live band."

*AMY MILLAN_* I remember Stars' first label meeting was with Virgin/EMI. All these people thought they were going to get fired because the record industry was going down, and they were all joking around about how the cards that let them into the building might not work when they showed up the next morning, and they were all going to get laid off — this was our introductory meeting to the label! We all left there feeling so gross.

WE WERE LEANING ON EACH OTHER, HELPING EACH OTHER MAKE MUSIC, AND BELIEVING IN ONE ANOTHER.

It was a really dark period for all of us. Metric had all these other deals — they always seemed like they were ahead — but then they kept getting dropped or their labels fell apart. We were leaning on each other, helping each other make music, and believing in one another. When I was in 16 Tons, I remember James and Emily and Kevin were the only people in the audience at one of our Ted's Wrecking Yard shows. We always had each other's backs.

*LESLIE FEIST_* I made *Monarch* around the same time By Divine Right made *Bless This Mess*. I did a double CD-release party at the Rivoli with Jim Guthrie, who I met through BDR — Goldy [By Divine Right drummer Mark Goldstein] was his biggest fan, and on all those BDR tours, all we listened to was Jimmy Guthrie. Then, through Jimmy, I met the Royal City crew, and they said, "Our friend Tyler Burke should draw your poster." She drew a poster that was like a playing card, with a king and a queen — me and Jim Guthrie — and we hung them all over the city upside down and right side up. Tyler had lots of crazy guerrilla tactics — we pulled over a car right in front of the MuchMusic building and quickly hung up a string across two trees. The invitations were in these sealed envelopes that we waxed shut with a red F. We hung up invitations to the gig with clothespins, right in front of MuchMusic, hoping someone would come. In every town [Royal City] played, Tyler and I would go around town all afternoon and hang up these clotheslines everywhere.

GENTLEMAN REG_ Three Gut Records started in Guelph. It was Aaron Riches and Jim Guthrie [of Royal City] and me and Tyler Clark Burke. It was a collective that lasted for a very short period. Lisa Moran worked for another record label, DROG, so Aaron brought her in. And then we all moved to Toronto, and that's when [the label's success] really began. We all felt we had to move to Toronto to make something happen.

TYLER CLARK BURKE_ We moved to Toronto and we were living in this accidental expat-Guelph community. I didn't know anyone in Toronto, so walking down the streets almost felt like a movie set, like it was all make-believe. On one hand, nobody would come to the shows; on the other hand, this disconnect was completely liberating. Maybe this is what inspired the envelope project. I had nothing to do with the music business, and at the time I had always been a bit of a math kid, and there was a problem in front of me. A logic problem, essentially. How do we interact with and entice the foreigner? If we could trick people with mischief, then we would all have fun. I would run around and string up lines of envelopes with the words OPEN ME stamped on them, sometimes in totally corporate

music environments, and I'd just hide and watch how people responded to the message inside. I felt like an anthropologist watching people's behaviour. The one Leslie and I set up was a joint show for her and Jim Guthrie. Normally thirty people would come to our shows, and after a week of these hijinks, there were hundreds of people showing up — strangers, some of them alone, some holding the envelope. It was amazing, and it was really the beginning.

LISA MORAN_ Tyler threw this crazy loft-party — the "Aliens Have Landed" Three Gut launch [in August 2000] — and that was when I realized there were so many people at the party who wanted to help out, and also so many strangers who seemed excited and interested in what was going on. The shows started getting bigger too. In the beginning, we knew everyone who was at the show, and all of a sudden I looked around and thought, "Who are these people?" Or we'd see strangers on the street in Three Gut T-shirts.

TYLER CLARK BURKE_ At the beginning of Three Gut, I was just waking up from a long sleep. I had been really ill for seven years and bedridden for long periods of time. When I started to get better, I had so much energy and so much time to make up for. And I kept meeting the most incredible people. I lived in this warehouse on Portland with this gang of people I knew through Aaron and his old hardcore days, and there was this warehouse across the courtyard and downstairs. I think there were thirteen people living there communally — [public-space activist] Dave Meslin was one of them, and [artists] Sandy Plotnikoff, Rose Bianchini — it was a wild group, and I felt at home. We had the best courtyard, and we decided to throw a party together. I was building sets, ideas, little characters, big walls of colour. None of us actually really thought about who would come, and

Steve Lambke and Bry Webb of the Constantines performing at Bar Code in Toronto, 2001. (TCB)

Jim Guthrie, 2000. (TCB)

Lisa Moran and Gentleman Reg, 2000. (TCB)

RADIO MONDAY
hosted by Jason Collet

Feb. 5

KEVIN DREW &
CHARLES SPEARIN
of broken social scene

JUSTIN SMALL
of do make say think

JOEL GIBB
of hidden cameras

BOB WISEMAN

Feb. 12

TORQUIL   of
CAMPBELL   stars

LESLIE FEIST

the BICYCLES

REID JAMESON

Feb. 19

TANNIS SLIMON

RUBY DRAKE

RON HAWKINS

Feb. 26

BRYAN WEbb
of constantines

GENTLEMAN RE

bRIAN bORCHER

Radio Monday poster, Toronto, 2001. (JPF)

then, somehow, thousands of people came. It was really magical, and I threw this energy into everything in my life, like Three Gut: a label with no records, no distribution, no money — just a logo and a pile of antics. It's easy to start something when you don't know any of the rules. All that mattered was sharing music and having fun house shows and community.

***LESLIE FEIST*_** Royal City was one of my little islands of peace. I played with them for maybe a summer, but I didn't really feel like I was a member and I was losing my steam in general. Aaron was really serious about the band at the time. I was in Regina visiting my grandma, and he would call and say, "You have to come back for this photo shoot!" It just felt like the scales were tipping and I was doing less music and more and more phone calls, so I kind of pressed Pause and went inward. I four-tracked a lot and started making what would become the Red Demos [which formed the basis for 2004's *Let It Die*]. That was right around the same time Peaches moved to Berlin. She was over there for twenty minutes before she called me and said, "I'm sending you a ticket to Vienna and I want you to come on tour with me."

***JOHN CROSSINGHAM*_** For so long, I was trying to get away from that Sebadoh/Pavement/Guided by Voices lo-fi indie-rock thing, as much as I love those bands. I wanted to be a better singer; I wanted music that was a little more emotive and personal. And I found it in Toronto. Even though Raising the Fawn were from St. Catharines and we didn't sound like Royal City or K.C. Accidental, there was a sense that a lot of bands were focusing on music that was about a sense of tranquility and a sense of quiet and underplaying and a minimalist aesthetic. I had gotten to know the guys in Royal City and people like Jonny Bunce. So I was feeling more and more in touch with Toronto as a city, as opposed to this place

I liked to visit but also scared the shit out of me — too expensive, too big.

***JONATHAN BUNCE[1]*_** The Toronto scene was splintered into little social cliques that were barely aware of each other's existences. The shows consisted of three or four bands who were friends with each other playing to each other and their friends. Insularity leads to stagnation and by late 1999, a group of us got together and decided we needed to take action to create some excitement and energy. Our bands — Parts Unknown, Neck, Mean Red Spiders, Mason Hornet, Kid Sniper — had been playing shows together for about six years at that point, and still no one else seemed to know or care. There was so much other music happening in the city that excited me — the free-jazz improv, experimental electronic, garage-rock and basement hardcore scenes — and I felt we had to cross-pollinate to survive, find the interesting spots where the circles overlap — that's where culture evolves. Hence, the Wavelength night was consciously "curated," putting together bands who might otherwise never share a stage together, but might hopefully find some common ground.

***STEVE LAMBKE[2]*_** I don't think it's possible to overstate how important Wavelength's been to new Toronto indie bands — it's been a very awesome thing for the city.

***JOHN CROSSINGHAM*_** The first thing I remember Kevin Drew saying to me was when we were rehearsing a song for sound check and him saying, "Sounds good." This was the Raising the Fawn/John Tesh Jr./Russian Futurists show at Wavelength in December 2000. I liked Kevin's set a lot — I remember Brian Cram from GUH came up and played a little horn. His set was a lot of keyboard drones, really ambient and very typical of his contributions to the K.C. Accidental and first Broken

Social Scene records: these Eno-esque soundscapes. I was starting to feel a sense of early but strong confidence about what was I doing. I was always really intimidated by Toronto, but Raising the Fawn was doing more and more shows up here, and finally getting into that bigger thing that always felt like it would never happen, like playing North by Northeast or getting press in *Exclaim!* or *Eye Weekly* — things like that, for a St. Catharines band, felt really good. I felt a little bit more a part of a community. Lisa Moran and Tyler Burke from Three Gut Records were both really supportive initially.

GENTLEMAN REG_ Tyler and Lisa were super-good at creating attention. Tyler had a lot of amazing ideas, and Royal City did pretty well off the bat. They did a lot of U.S. stuff and they had a lot of luck — like, Robert Munsch wrote this book [*Aaron's Hair*] based on Aaron Riches, and weird little things like that got extra attention for people. And then Three Gut signed Constantines, who blew up immediately.

I REMEMBER KEVIN BEING REALLY DRUNK, AND I DIDN'T KNOW HIM. AND THEN I PLAYED "GIVE ME A CHANCE TO FALL" — THIS TWO-MINUTE POP SONG — AND THEN KEVIN COERCED ME TO PLAY THE SONG AGAIN. AND THAT WAS THE BEGINNING OF OUR RELATIONSHIP.

BRY WEBB[3]_ It's bizarre . . . my faith in indie shows and underground music has resurfaced with a lot of energy. [Constantines] played these shows in new cities where we haven't played before, and people are coming out like crazy. The turnout we got at the Raven in Hamilton or Ted's Wrecking Yard in Toronto was amazing. It seems like the Wavelength series is really doing things right. Maybe there was a little dry spell when a lot of people weren't coming to shows but it definitely seems like the excitement is coming back. People are starting to really support underground music and allowing themselves to get enthusiastic.

GENTLEMAN REG_ I got connected with The Hidden Cameras through [his friends] Justin Stayshyn and Maghali Meager, because they were from Guelph and they were in this new, exciting band.

JOEL GIBB[4]_ I was pretty much new to everything in terms of the art scene, and doing anything other than school was pretty exciting to me. When I started the band [in 2000], that's when I moved out of Mississauga. Toronto was a very accepting place for new stuff, for new art, for new ideas. Our first show was in an art gallery. I've never had a band before and I was forming it, so I could create my own process and my own aesthetic or universe. Why give all this money and business to a bar, when we can do something really cool on our own?

GENTLEMAN REG_ There were so many things The Hidden Cameras did that you see in other bands like Arcade Fire: a lot of the performative aspects, a lot of the audience interaction. . . . We used to have a member that just banged on a floor tom. But for some reason, I feel like the Cameras aren't getting credit; I feel like nobody knows that about them. When I moved here, the only people I knew were from Guelph, and they were all straight indie-rock kids, so the Cameras were my gateway to the art and queer scene of Toronto, like [queer rock 'n' roll dance night] Vazaleen. It was magical.

JONATHAN BUNCE_ Those who move to downtown Toronto usually stay here for a long time. They are usually well-educated and open-minded, have huge, diverse record and book collections, and absorb some of the most astounding cultural diversity in the world. American indie scenes, in contrast, are often born in high-turnover college towns that are correspondingly more transient and trend-driven — and you're considered old at twenty-four there. I like the fact that it's not so weird for people in T.O. indie bands to be pushing forty.

*JASON COLLETT_* I stopped trying [to get a record deal] and started doing the Radio Monday night, which was in the spirit of what was going on in the city; Wavelength had that spirit of just doing it locally and celebrating what was immediate. Radio Monday was an extension of what happened at my house a lot — we had a lot of impromptu parties and all-night around-the-kitchen-table song sharing. The idea was to take that intimacy into a small club with a simple songwriter-in-the-round format. I was really into the experience of playing music without the audience in mind and was more focused on sharing new material with artists. The real magic happened when a couple of friends joined in on a chorus and you could hear a harmony for the first time. Often, those moments an audience never sees. So the audience would get a glimpse of the more vulnerable, intimate parts of [being] artists that would normally be on display in the comfort and privacy of their band.

*GENTLEMAN REG_* I was playing a Radio Monday at Rancho Relaxo with Jason Collett, Kevin Drew, Joel Gibb, and Steve Singh. I remember Joel and I were feeling nervous and out of place and extra gay or something. I remember Kevin being really drunk, and I didn't know him. And then I played "Give Me a Chance to Fall" — this two-minute pop song — and then Kevin coerced me to play the song again. And that was the beginning of our relationship. There was a Broken Social Scene show at Lula Lounge [in December 2002] where Kevin asked me to come down and play my song, and again coerced me to play it twice. I went on to play that song twice with Broken Social Scene about twelve or fifteen times, and all over too: in New York, Austin, Montreal, Ottawa . . .

*JASON COLLETT_* I saw the Toronto scene change at that point. I've never had my finger on the pulse of the scene at any point in its history, because I've always been a domestic guy with a family. But from what I've been able to observe, the cynicism of the Toronto scene changed from being the most competitive place in the country — because it's got the biggest concentration of industry here — into being something I've always seen in cities like Guelph or Halifax: really community focused, where artists really supported one another. What started to dominate the flavour of the city was a real excitement for something that was passionate and dynamic. I don't think it was just music; it was like that in film and art as well. The city [had] reached a critical mass in population, where it was finally dense enough to be truly urban, and the sparks were ignited.

Leslie Feist playing with Royal City, 2000. (TCB)

Tyler Clark Burke at the Tequila Lounge, Toronto, 2002. (TCB)

LOVE AND MATHE- MATICS

FEEL GOOD LOST
TURNS TWO INTO TWELVE

MOST NEW FRIENDS get to know each other through drinks and conversation; Kevin Drew and Brendan Canning made *Feel Good Lost* instead. But as much as the album's cerebral instrumental tracks capture the feel of a new relationship forming — as heard in the comforting slow-motion embrace of songs like "I Slept with Bonhomme at CBC" and "Love and Mathematics" — *Feel Good Lost* also serves as an analogue for a Toronto music community that was just starting to wake up to its own potential. The album's meditative first eleven tracks effectively conjure the sense of hibernation and subterranean retreat that characterized the indie community at the turn of the millennium, before the joyous, brass-blasted finale "Cranley's Going to Make It" heralds the new era of celebratory communalism.

The first Broken Social Scene album was recorded in the basement of the house Drew shared with his wife, Jo-Ann Goldsmith, mixed by Do Make Say Think's Ohad Benchetrit and Charles Spearin, and mastered by Canning's old hHead comrade Noah Mintz, and featured guest appearances by an increasingly familiar group of friends: Justin Peroff, Leslie Feist, Evan Cranley, and Bill Priddle. *Feel Good Lost* was actually the second album Brendan Canning put out in 2001; his concurrent dance-music project, Cookie Duster (with Change of Heart's Bernard Maeizza), also released its debut album, with guest contributions from Danko Jones and By Divine Right's Jose Contreras. But it soon became clear that Canning would have time for only one band.

Canning is seven years Drew's senior, but their birthdays are just a day apart — September 6 and 7 respectively. Both possess a Virgo's sharp critical faculty, to the point where — even before *Feel Good Lost*'s February 2001 release on Noise Factory Records — the duo already knew they wanted to be a different kind of band than that first record documents. Like so many in Toronto, Drew and Canning were invigorated by the energy that labels like Three Gut Records and bands like The Hidden Cameras were injecting into the city. The sight of two guys onstage playing brooding instrumentals just wasn't going to cut it in this new participatory culture. **The summer of 2000 had seen Drew and Canning first perform together at Ted's Wrecking Yard alongside various friends in nameless aggregates.** The first properly billed Broken Social Scene show happened January 26, 2001, at Ted's Wrecking Yard — the club that effectively served as their centre of operations for the year — with Justin Peroff, Feist, and new addition Andrew Whiteman, who was a weekly resident at Ted's downstairs neighbour, Barcode, as his new, Cuban-influenced alter ego the Apostle of Hustle. And as was the case with every show Broken Social Scene played that year, not a single *Feel Good Lost* track was performed live. Instead, the band was recast as psychedelic lovers' rock, with the heretofore silent Drew assuming an increasingly prominent vocal presence. At this point they were already unveiling the songs that would later become their signatures, including "Lovers Spit."

Throughout the year, Broken Social Scene shows and set lists changed in conjunction with their expanding membership. Their April 2001 set at Kathedral for the *Exclaim!* party found them playing an ambient space-rock set behind a screen of video images projected by Christopher Mills, who was part of a small network of BSS-affiliated filmmakers that also included Eric Yealland, Stephen Chung, and Canning's new roommate, George Vale. That summer, Drew temporarily renamed the band Do the 95 to open a Rivoli gig for Jason Collett; they performed a handful of new songs purposely written to emulate '90s indie-rock icons like Pavement and Dinosaur Jr. When Broken Social Scene played Ted's Wrecking Yard in September, there were twelve people onstage, with a four-piece horn section mediating between the band's raucous energy and its grandiose ambitions.

If Broken Social Scene shows during this era featured all the shambling structure and accidental genius of a practice-space jam, it's because they were essentially practice-space jams — the stage being the only practice space big enough to accommodate them.

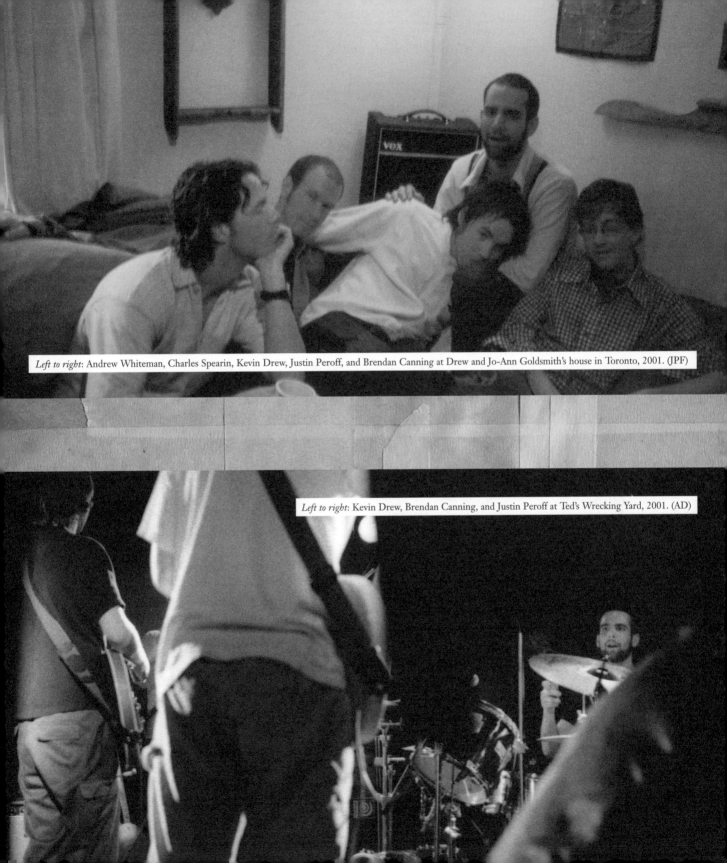

Left to right: Andrew Whiteman, Charles Spearin, Kevin Drew, Justin Peroff, and Brendan Canning at Drew and Jo-Ann Goldsmith's house in Toronto, 2001. (JPF)

Left to right: Kevin Drew, Brendan Canning, and Justin Peroff at Ted's Wrecking Yard, 2001. (AD)

CHARLES SPEARIN_ I went away for four months in 1999 for the first Do Makes tour in Europe, and then I went to Nepal afterward. I gave my eight-track to Kevin, which he set up in his basement, and when I got back he said, "I've fallen in love with this guy Brendan." I listened to a cassette copy of their record and I thought, "Wow, this is really great." They asked me to help mix, so we went into Ohad's studio and mixed the album.

KEVIN DREW[1]_ For me, it all started after the second K.C. Accidental record, when Justin Small [of Do Make Say Think] said, "Kevin you've got to find a band, find a bunch of musicians, and play with them." And Brendan walked in . . . I was about to do a bunch of recordings in a basement that I just moved into; I was going to build a studio, and while the Do Makes were on tour, they lent me their gear. That's when Canning and I made *Feel Good Lost* together.

> I LISTENED TO IT AND THOUGHT IT WAS REALLY SPECIAL. WE CAME BACK, HE DECIDED IT WAS GOING TO BE CALLED BROKEN SOCIAL SCENE, AND IT GETS RELEASED THROUGH NOISE FACTORY RECORDS.

JO-ANN GOLDSMITH_ Brendan was like the second wife in our relationship. He basically lived at our house; he watched movies with us, cooked for us. When we moved into our house, we made sure there was a big studio space downstairs that Kevin could play music in, and he would have the entire place to himself. It was kind of like a courting thing — Brendan and Kevin courted each other for a little while. He came over for dinner and they talked about the music they liked. And that was it — Brendan was over all the time making music in the basement.

JUSTIN PEROFF_ In fall of 2000, Charlie asked me, "Do you want to come to Europe with Do Make Say Think?" Dave Mitchell and Ohad Benchetrit had to stay home for work, so I filled in for Dave, and Kevin was asked to play keyboards for Ohad. I remember, on the plane, Kevin handed me a CD and it said "Broken Membership." I listened to it and thought it was really special. We came back, he decided it was going to be called Broken Social Scene, and it gets released through Noise Factory Records.

TORQUIL CAMPBELL_ My favourite Broken record is *Feel Good Lost* — it's the first time anybody ever made Toronto sound beautiful.

CHARLES SPEARIN_ You listen to K.C. Accidental and *Feel Good Lost* and you can tell they're coming from the same place. But Brendan has a totally different history in music and has his own influences. He's much more aware of what's going on in music than I am. Both Kevin and Brendan have PhDs in popular culture — they know all the movies and all the actors and all the bands. Brendan brought a bit more of an informed perspective to the thing. I love long-winded songs, but there were times when I was working on K.C. Accidental and Kevin would just keep going and going and going.

As we started rehearsing, we couldn't figure out if the album was going to be by K.C. Accidental or Broken Social Scene. We decided in the end that it couldn't be a K.C. Accidental project, because the contributions weren't just [being] made by Kevin and Charlie anymore. And Broken Social Scene seemed to fit the description of what we were doing more accurately.

NOAH MINTZ_ I thought out of Brendan's bands, Cookie Duster was actually more accessible than Broken Social Scene at the time. Spookey Ruben, Danko Jones, and Jose Contreras made guest appearances on the Cookie Duster album, so the record seemed to have a little more potential. But Bernard was agoraphobic — I don't think Cookie

an evening for whatever...

brendan canning
justin peroff
bill priddle
charles spearin
kevin drew
leslie feist

firday april 28th @
ted's wrecking yard

A flyer advertising a pre-BSS concert at Ted's Wrecking Yard, 2000. (KD)

Justin Peroff on drums at Ted's Wrecking Yard, 2001. (AD)

Kevin Drew and Jo-Ann Goldsmith, 2001. (SC)

Front to back: Charles Spearin, Andrew Whiteman, and Kevin Drew at Ted's Wrecking Yard, 2001. This photo became the cover image for the original edition of Broken Social Scene's 2002 album, *You Forgot It In People*. (AD)

BRENDAN AND KEVIN AND I WERE PART OF THE SAME SOCIAL SCENE — WE WENT TO THE SAME KIND OF PARTIES, AND WE WERE ALL LEARNING ABOUT BEAT CULTURE AND ECSTASY CULTURE.

Kevin Drew on keyboard and Brendan Canning on bass performing at Ted's Wrecking Yard, 2001. (AD)

Duster ever played a live show. *Feel Good Lost* was a good album, but I didn't really think much of it. I thought it was a kind of electronic album you listened to while taking E.

CHRISTOPHER MILLS_ Brendan and Kevin and I were part of the same social scene — we went to the same kind of parties, and we were all learning about beat culture and ecstasy culture. We were influenced by the kind of music we listened to after a party to make ourselves feel good: bands from Chicago — The Sea and Cake and Tortoise — and we also discovered Four Tet. We would go to a crazy party, it would reach a euphoric end or a dark place, and then you'd listen to music afterward to make you feel better. Broken Social Scene made the kind of music you listened to to get back into your life.

JUSTIN PEROFF_ Brendan and Kevin started writing in Kevin's basement with the usual suspects who were involved with K.C., as well as other people like Bill Priddle and Feist. You look at the list of guests on *Feel Good Lost* and you have the foreshadowing of the live band.

LESLIE FEIST_ Kevin was this kid who had come to one of our 701 parties. I thought he was gay because he had a guy on his lap the whole time, but then I heard he was married, and I was like, "Whoa." And I always thought he was a kid because he looked so young. I remember him saying, "Hey, my wife will teach you yoga if you teach us singing." And I was just like, "Who is this guy?" And then a few days later Canning was like, "Come over, I want you to sing on this project I'm doing with this guy," and I arrived and Kevin was that guy. So that was how we made "Passport Radio."

BILL PRIDDLE_ We started jamming in Kevin's basement with Justin, Charles, and Brendan. There was no songwriting because everyone seemed to be in a contest: "Oh, you think you can play the same thing? Well, I can play the same thing longer."

ERIC YEALLAND_ I've known Whitey since I was seventeen, and I've always really liked him personally and his musical style and his attitude toward music and art in general — he's just a very passionate person. And I saw a similar, though very different, passion in Kevin. Once they hooked up, they ran with it.

ANDREW WHITEMAN_ I would occasionally run into Eric Yealland, and he kept telling me about this kid Kevin Drew. Eric just knew. I met Kevin at Eric's, and that was the first time I heard Tortoise — I didn't know about that whole post-rock thing. I didn't know Do Makes. Right around Christmas 2000, there was a Stars gig at Ted's, and I went with Feist. Emily and Jimmy were playing with Stars, and that was my first time meeting all those people. Kevin was taking care of Eric's house, so after that night we all went back there and jammed. I was going out with Feist; we went to Cuba and came back, and then it was like, "These guys want to do a show, and you should play in the band."

LESLIE FEIST_ The power of Brendan and Kevin finding each other was pretty intense. They were like a complete symbiosis of each other. And personality-wise they complemented each other perfectly: Canning is so chill, and Kevin's such a sparkplug.

ANDREW WHITEMAN_ Feist hated Kevin at first because he wouldn't let her play guitar, and that rubbed her the wrong way.

THE POWER OF BRENDAN AND KEVIN FINDING EACH OTHER WAS PRETTY INTENSE. THEY WERE LIKE A COMPLETE SYMBIOSIS OF EACH OTHER.

Left to right: Justin Peroff, Brendan Canning, John Crossingham, Charles Spearin, and Andrew Whiteman performing at Ted's Wrecking Yard, 2001. (AD)

Brendan Canning and Kevin Drew, 2000. (SC)

*LESLIE FEIST_* I identified myself as a guitar player, but I wasn't a good guitar player by their standards. At one jam, Kevin came up behind me and grabbed my arms and pretended I was a puppet, saying, "I'm not gonna bring my guitar tomorrow!" And I thought, "Okay, that's his way of telling me I'm not up to snuff." So my opinion changed on what my role was going to be in this band. I realized that, since I wasn't going to play guitar anymore, I was going to sing a couple of songs every now and then. I guess it changed my level of security/commitment. I was trying to get the chance to play the guitar next to Charles Spearin, who was blowing my mind, and Priddle was there, and we were making these beautiful noise sculptures. So to be told, "No, you're not going to play guitar anymore," was like saying, "You're not invited to trick-or-treat with us." But there are no hard feelings . . . and Kevin hates that I remember this story.

*KEVIN DREW_* In the middle of a *Feel Good Lost* session with Brendan, I started busting into some Bernard Sumner/New Order lines, and he said to me, "You know what, you've got to sing." But all I knew how to do was sing like J Mascis, Neil Young, and Kermit the Frog. I hated singing. I hated that I had to think about what I was going to say. And I never wanted a voice to tell you the story. I wanted the audience to evoke whatever emotion they needed to from the music.

But there were three things that made me sing. One, I always enjoyed singers. Two, I was a massive Jeff Buckley fan. Three, I met Feist. And at the time we were going to do a show together, and she said, "You should sing this song." I was not a singer but someone who sang from the stomach. The most glorious thing I will take from our relationship is this admiration I have for her voice. It broke barriers for me, because I was able to take what I love about all of my favourite singers and see it in somebody that I knew.

*LESLIE FEIST_* Kevin was like the Midas-touch kingpin. I look back on that time now and it was like an improv movie with Kevin as the director. Kevin — who had never toured in his life and had only played a handful of gigs at The Mockingbird — had these guys who had made tons of albums. Whitey had written these Big Sugar hits, I had already toured for how many years, Canning was with hHead and had already gone through the cycle. And Kevin was telling them what to do. He opened a door to a new era for all these people. All of us were doing stuff we had never tried before. I remember we jammed at the 701 a few times, and we ran into Yvonne [the booking agent at Ted's Wrecking Yard] one night and said, "Let's book a show. We'll write the songs for that show, and we'll play each other's songs and see who's around and wants to do it. Let's just start it as a winter project." We didn't play any *Feel Good Lost* songs that first night.

*YVONNE MATSELL_* Ted's Wrecking Yard was a well-loved room, even though there was a lot wrong with it — I believe there was only one toilet functioning at a time, with caution tape on the door.

*ANDREW WHITEMAN_* We made up these tunes, which became a tradition. We performed four Feist tunes, one song that I was sort of working on, and then we made up a few. Feist was distracted because she was in a fight with Royal City over some grant stuff. Meanwhile, [among] me and my new buds — Canning, Drew, and Peroff — there was love. We walked offstage when we were finished, looked at each other, and said, "Wow, when's the next show?"

> *THE MOST GLORIOUS THING I WILL TAKE FROM OUR RELATIONSHIP IS THIS ADMIRATION I HAVE FOR HER VOICE. IT BROKE BARRIERS FOR ME, BECAUSE I WAS ABLE TO TAKE WHAT I LOVE ABOUT ALL OF MY FAVOURITE SINGERS AND SEE IT IN SOMEBODY THAT I KNEW.*

***JOHN CROSSINGHAM*_** I got a job at Soundscapes in January 2001, and we received the promo copy of *Feel Good Lost* and it was getting quite a lot of play in the shop. Kevin came into the store and he asked, "How's the Raising the Fawn record coming along?" He started listening to a copy I had, skipped through a couple of tracks, and said, "That's a nice change there . . . Did you play everything yourself?" And I said, "Yeah." And then he said, "Well, we're putting together a live band — do you want to be a part of it?" At the time I was asked to be a drummer, because he and Peroff were having a falling-out — one of several. But I eventually started playing more guitar. My first show with Broken Social Scene was at an *Exclaim!* party at Kathedral [in April 2001].

BROKEN SOCIAL SCENE IS REALLY A TEAM OF THIRTY PEOPLE AND CROSSES THE BORDER INTO PHOTOGRAPHY, VIDEO, ARTWORK — WE WANT TO START SOMETHING THAT OFFERS MORE THAN JUST MUSIC.

***YVONNE MATSELL*_** The shows were always fascinating because the band never played the same old set. The crowd seemed to grow and love the performances. Anything original and creative like that is going to pique your interest. If I book a band on a regular basis, the set's usually going to have the same material. How can you not like that something's developing before your eyes? It's thrilling.

***CHARLES SPEARIN*_** Every song was new. We would just jam in Kevin and Jo-Ann's basement and we'd come up with ten great songs, and we'd feel great. Some of the shows we did were great and some of them were not. I remember one show at the Kathedral. The first ten minutes were fantastic, and then it just went on and on for a long, long time.

***BILL PRIDDLE*_** I always thought it was insane, but they wouldn't play any songs from the record.

***JOE ENGLISH*_** It was frustrating for me, because as a label I had been putting out music and I hadn't had anybody touring, which is an essential part of selling albums. And then finally I get a band that played live, and then they don't play any of the songs on their record! I wasn't really into the full-on rock show. My interests were going in different ways — I was listening to more minimal techno stuff at the time, like Richie Hawtin and Pole. So when Kevin was playing more of the rock music, I was like, "That's okay, I've heard it before."

***NOAH MINTZ*_** I saw them every time they played. The one show I really remembered was at Ted's and they played behind a movie screen. And they had all the different musicians playing, and it was the first time it felt like a collective, because it wasn't so important who was on stage.

***KEVIN DREW*[2]_** Broken Social Scene is really a team of thirty people and crosses the border into photography, video, artwork — we want to start something that offers more than just music. It's our loved ones and it's all our friends. We didn't do this on our own.

***CHRISTOPHER MILLS*_** It sounds kind of hypey, but I don't think that [statement] is bullshit. It felt like the making of a different kind of work would be an antidote to all the trouble we got into. You sin for a while, you do drugs, and then you want to make up for those sins, and atone for the trouble you got into and turn it into something productive. I did visuals for a few Do Make Say Think shows, and that's how I started working with Broken Social Scene. I wanted to play around with a translucent screen and visuals up front, so everything would blend together. I was pretty good at guessing the flavour of the night and putting together a whole pile of VHS tapes at my side, and making them match what was going on onstage. If

I was involved in shooting their live shows, it was only because I didn't know how to play guitar and wanted to contribute.

GEORGE VALE_ I moved into Brendan Canning's house on Draper Street in 2000. I had moved to L.A. and directed Alice in Chains' last video, I did videos for Sponge, Fuel . . . I was doing big, glossy, overproduced bands, but when I got back here, what I was looking for was right there in front of me. Broken Social Scene was movie music — very cinematic, visual music.

EVAN CRANLEY_ It was an incredible time: ten people on stage improvising every night. We'd just start from nothing. Brendan would start with a lovely Wurlitzer part and then we'd build these great jams. I came up with this guitar called a two-tar — because there were so many great guitar players in the band, the only way I could really cut through was to invent this guitar that had only two strings. Instead of just adding to the curtain of sound, I could poke through with these little hooks. That was a great experience for me; I could do the brass arrangements and be part of the moody side of things, but I could also get involved in the rock 'n' roll side doing the two-tar.

JOHN CROSSINGHAM_ Kevin was really coming into his own as a singer. He had a great instinct for it; he was just a little unsure of how his voice would come across or how much it collided with the aesthetic that he had put in place for the band, which was this faceless identity — a bunch of musicians onstage, playing behind screens and projections, with a lot of improvisation. Out of a thirteen-song show, there might be four songs with significant vocals, and some of those would be split with Emily or Feist. For a little while Kevin wanted to separate [the pop and instrumental material] by having that Do the 95 band, where the concept was just the

Social Scene crew as a rock band, playing Dinosaur Jr. heavy shit.

JUSTIN PEROFF_ We had planned a rehearsal and no one could make it, but I showed up. Me and Kevin ended up being in the basement at the same time and he said to me, "I'm not happy right now — I'm angry!" We started playing really heavy shit, and then one of us said, "This is like doing the '95" because it was all circa 1995–type indie-rock music. Some of those songs, like "Cause," became Social Scene songs.

IT WAS AN INCREDIBLE TIME: TEN PEOPLE ON STAGE IMPROVISING EVERY NIGHT. WE'D JUST START FROM NOTHING.

EVAN CRANLEY_ The band will always have that Ted's Wrecking Yard ethereal quality, but when we did Do the 95, that's when the pop songs came together. Broken Social Scene became those two bands with the recording of *You Forgot It In People*.

JAMES SHAW_ After Emily and I came back from England to New York at the end of 2000, we would also spend a bunch of time in Toronto, and something happened after those Ted's shows. I remember saying to Kev, "You've got something — go make a record. What's happening on that stage is awesome." I remember there was this pivotal meeting at the Clear Spot, and he invited all the people he thought would be involved. That's when we all thought, "Okay, we might have to do something about this."

KEVIN DREW_ I had a serious drive. And so did Charlie and Justin — we just wanted to be involved in something good. Charlie was already a part of something good [Do Make Say Think]; he wanted to continue that. Brendan had been there, done that. So had Whitey. They had their run trying to prove themselves out there. Whitey did two runs —

THERE WAS JUST A SENSE THAT THERE WAS STRENGTH IN THIS SCENE, AND EVERYONE BELIEVED THEY COULD DO MORE WITH THE MUSIC THEY WERE CREATING.

Broken Social Scene performing at the *Exclaim!* Anniversary Party at Kathedral, 2001. (SC)

he did the Bourbons, he did Que Vida — and so he said, "I've had a few cracks. I'm outta here." When we met Andrew, he was planning to move to Spain. And then once we started playing, I turned to him and said, "You can't move to Spain. You just can't. Why? Because this is going to happen."

JOHN CROSSINGHAM_ You had people who were going for another crack, in some cases the third or fourth time around. There was just a sense that there was strength in this scene, and everyone believed they could do more with the music they were creating. They stopped looking to the outside for inspiration and instead turned toward their friends.

BRENDAN CANNING_ Finally, I had a group that was like an all-star cast and had focus.

THEY ALL WANT TO BE THE CAUSE

MEMORIES OF
YOU FORGOT IT IN PEOPLE

IF JUSTIN PEROFF hadn't gotten dumped by a girlfriend in 2001, you might never have heard of Broken Social Scene and I wouldn't have written this book. But what was bad for Justin's love life proved to be crucial to the band's eventual success, as the breakup initiated a series of occurrences that would lead Broken Social Scene to Dave Newfeld's Stars and Sons studios. And believe me, you needed all the help you could get to find the place, which was tucked away on Cameron Street, a dark, desolate laneway best known for boozecans and muggers. That the studio boasted little in the way of natural light was of small concern to Newfeld, given that he mostly worked through the night and made his bed in the studio's windowless boiler room.

Broken Social Scene entered Stars and Sons in January 2002, stayed for three months, and later returned to complete recording and mixing in July. What made Broken Social Scene shows so exciting at the time was their sense of inspired randomness. But when divorced from the euphoria of live performance, that mercurial quality could just as easily come off as aimless and indecisive. It remained to be seen how an urgent rock song like "Cause = Time" could coexist alongside the breezy bossa nova–tinged balladry of "Looks Just Like the Sun" and a dramatic, dub-inspired set piece like "Shampoo Suicide" (né "Fuzz Song").

Newfeld, a wedding DJ by trade, was the only producer crazy enough to try to make sense of this musical mess. His trick was to harness Justin Peroff's rhythms as precise, mechanistic movements while immersing the melodies in a surface mist of ambient textures. The end result was not a document of a Broken

Social Scene performance but a dream of one, where the juxtapositions felt initially sudden, yet ultimately natural.

You Forgot It In People was released in October 2002 and immediately received five-star reviews in *Eye Weekly*, *NOW* magazine, and the *Toronto Sun*; the first run of 1,000 copies sold out in less than a month. Meanwhile, Feist went off to resume her solo career in Paris, Charles Spearin shifted his focus back to Do Make Say Think, and James Shaw and Emily Haines relocated Metric to L.A. to work more closely with their new label, Restless Records. Broken Social Scene fortified their ranks with Stars' Amy Millan, new full-time member Jason Collett, and part-time violinist Julie Penner. Following a sold-out CD release show at Lula Lounge in December 2002, Broken Social Scene would be a strictly Toronto phenomenon no longer.

eye
WEEKLY

ARTS
Official ethnic jokes 48

NEWS Funny finances redo Union Station

CITY Collecting art on a budget 16

DECEMBER 12, 2002

Broken Social Scene on the cover of the December 12, 2002, edition of *Eye Weekly*. (PW)

KEVIN DREW[1]_ There were already enough records out there from friends of ours that were doing something different, so I didn't want to do what they were doing. The Do Makes slowly killed the ideology of playing instrumentals for me, because I was just so close to them and they do it so well, and I just thought, "I don't want to make an instrumental record now. I want to bring something else to this lovely circle of music." The Hidden Cameras, Gentleman Reg, Deep Dark United, Constantines — if you put all those bands on a stage, you're going to hear something different from each band, and I wanted to get on that stage and do something different from those people. They were the ones who inspired us to do this stuff.

I ENDED UP DATING A GIRL ON THIS TV SHOW I WAS DOING — I TOTALLY FELL IN LOVE, AND TOTALLY GOT MY HEART BROKEN. I REALLY WANTED A DISTRACTION. SO ME AND MY FRIEND DYLAN HUDECKI — WHO WAS THEN PLAYING IN BY DIVINE RIGHT — WERE TALKING AND HE SAID, "LET'S MAKE MUSIC TOGETHER."

OHAD BENCHETRIT_ Kevin's a smart guy; he's got his finger on the pulse of a lot of things. Maybe he realized at the time that [*You Forgot It In People*] was getting made that he had to use his other influences and other leanings to break through a scene that was already hitting its apex. Early Broken Social Scene had a strong tie with the kind of post-rock music that was being made then. But he shifted gears, and it was obviously the right way to go.

JUSTIN PEROFF_ I ended up dating a girl on this TV show I was doing — I totally fell in love, and totally got my heart broken. I really wanted a distraction. So me and my friend Dylan Hudecki — who was then playing in By Divine Right — were talking and he said, "Let's make music together." We started recording our *Junior Blue* album on Cubase at his house, and he said, "I know a guy we can record drums with," and that was Dave Newfeld at Stars and Sons.

DAVE NEWFELD_ I was just trying to make records. It was never a career; I was going to make music whether I was successful or not. [At the time] I was producing dance or computer-based music; I wasn't really working with bands. But then I started making records with the Mean Red Spiders and Neck. I thought, "I'm going to record bands that I think are cool." I had opened Stars and Sons in '98 — the studio got that name because it says H. STARR & SONS on the door. It was a bookbinding place.

ANDREW WHITEMAN_ I remember going in there with Newf, and right away I was like, "Holy fuck, how does this guy make the drums sound so good? He should be making dance music — he is a master of the drums and rhythms because he's a wedding DJ!"

DAVE NEWFELD_ That's why I could have such a cheap studio. Five days a week I could be devoted to not making any money, but on the weekend I'd make $500 DJing. So I knew I'd at least have my expenses covered and stay afloat without having to devote Monday to Friday to getting that $500 a week.

ANDREW WHITEMAN_ At first, with Dave, I thought, "Oh my god, I've struck gold — he's an incredible drum-sounds guy!" And then you start to realize it's not going to be that easy. We're taking the Starship Enterprise journey: you can teleport in and out, but you can't really get off the ship.

DAVE NEWFELD_ Recording was a disaster at first, because I had done a lot of changes in my studio just before Broken Social Scene came in, and stuff was blowing up and had not been tested. One

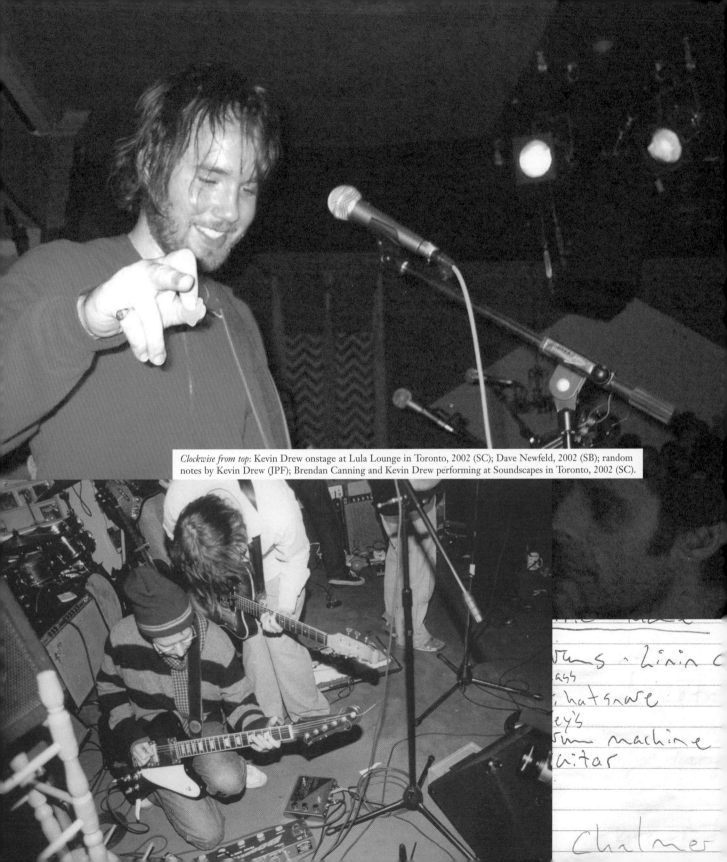

Clockwise from top: Kevin Drew onstage at Lula Lounge in Toronto, 2002 (SC); Dave Newfeld, 2002 (SB); random notes by Kevin Drew (JPF); Brendan Canning and Kevin Drew performing at Soundscapes in Toronto, 2002 (SC).

Poster promoting a Broken Social Scene and Stars concert at Lee's Palace, 2002. (JPF)

of the compressors had smoke coming out of the back. At first they were all freaked out, but by the second day we were rollin'. We had all these breakthroughs. We got "Stars and Sons," a wicked original song with Brendan singing lead vocals for the first time in his life. At that point everyone started feeling like, "Okay, we can call this place home, and good shit will happen here."

CHARLES SPEARIN_ I felt like I made 100,000 decisions on that record. There was Kevin, me, Brendan, and Newf working together, and then John Crossingham, Andrew Whiteman, and Justin Peroff were the next group, and then there were people who'd come in once in a while, like Evan Cranley and James Shaw. We were like the generals, the colonels, and the sergeants.

JAMES SHAW_ "Almost Crimes" is my clearest memory because it began as a whole other song. We're sitting there playing it and it was feeling really good, but Kevvy was sick as a dog. He was in the middle isolation room and you could hear him shivering on the microphone — he was dying. He kept saying, "No, it's not happening." And then all of a sudden I came up with that main riff, and he said, "That's good, keep going." Everyone just picked up on that, and all of a sudden we thought, "Holy shit, we've got to press Record right now." It was one of those moments where I felt like, "This is what I have to offer this band. This is it, right now." And then Crossingham walks in and says, "I think you guys took the song in the wrong direction. It's way too Strokesy." And I just remember looking up at him and saying, "Dude, get the fuck out of the room!"

CHARLES SPEARIN_ I wasn't there for the bedtracks of "Almost Crimes," but when I first heard it, I hated it. It sounded like a Dinosaur Jr./Strokes thing and it was a little too fashiony, so I laid all

these weird keyboards over it. This was before Feist came in to sing on it.

LESLIE FEIST_ In my mind, there are two eras. First was the genesis-of-an-idea era, and then there was the idea-becoming-a-band era. Even *You Forgot It In People* still felt like a genesis moment; the idea just went from the basement to the studio. Ideas were being thrown in the air and we were jamming, except we had the Record button on. I felt like Newf was a member of the band. He was the right kind of guy for us to be collaborating with. The door was always open to me; I was free to do anything I wanted — as long as it wasn't playing guitar.

At the same time, Peaches was saying to me, "Come over to Europe." So, for those couple of years, I had one foot in Toronto and one foot in Europe. I played all the Broken Social Scene shows, but I was in Europe most of the time. I comfort myself by saying that a lot of the spark-of-life stuff happened in the basement jamming — like "Almost Crimes" — and I was there for that. It didn't make me feel like less of a member to be coming and going, that's what the nature of the band was.

> *IDEAS WERE BEING THROWN IN THE AIR AND WE WERE JAMMING, EXCEPT WE HAD THE RECORD BUTTON ON.*

EMILY HAINES_ I got a call: "Emily, can you come down to the Horseshoe? We're doing this show — can you sing?" I had been working on "Anthems for a Seventeen-Year-Old Girl." We'd been in Kevin's basement, and Champ just played this line. I started coming up with something, and he just went, "How about something like, 'Used to be. . .'?" And then I spent the next three days walking around Toronto and writing those words. The repetition became this momentum, and I feel like that's my contribution to the band: the textural voice as an instrument. I heard the recording of

"Anthems for a Seventeen-Year-Old Girl" and I couldn't really hear myself in it, which is the classic Broken Social Scene move — everything is obscured behind the wall of marijuana. I don't remember having any sense that it was going to have a particular impact.

EVAN CRANLEY_ It was more like a recording project that turned into a record. Broken Social Scene was still very much an idea at that point. I remember doing "Almost Crimes" off the floor and thinking this was going to be a really special record. It definitely had a magic to it that I've never been a part of since. Everyone's really good at not stepping on each other's toes — you can't teach that. Newf was in a really great place too; he was just flowin'.

BRENDAN CANNING_ Going in, we had had "Capture the Flag" — Kevin demoed that song for a Bruce McDonald film [*Picture Claire*]. "KC Accidental" — that one we rehearsed in the basement. "Stars and Sons"— that song was written the first day of recording. "Looks Just Like the Sun" — we had played that one live, but worked on it a lot in the studio. "Anthems" was already written. "Late Nineties Bedroom Rock" — we worked on that song live. "Lovers Spit" and "Cause" were already written. "I'm Still Your Fag" was written in the studio. And we tried "Jimmy and the Photo Call" and "It's All Gonna Break."

KEVIN DREW[2]_ We didn't do any pre-production, which is apparently what you're supposed to do. We had seventeen songs on paper, and we chose fourteen. Newf never stopped pressing Record. He was the angel and the demon to everything, and those two sides got us through the making of the album. He put everything on the line for us, once we showed him we were worth it. His teeth were falling out when we were making this record — he couldn't eat except in one particular corner of his mouth he could chew. But he kept going, because he didn't have time to see the dentist. He wanted this record almost more than we did at times.

CHARLES SPEARIN_ I didn't really like Newf at first too much, because he was kind of taking my job! I was the engineer, and I just wanted to get to a place where we could afford good gear. We didn't want a producer going in at all. But as the recording went along, I let him go a bit more because I liked a lot of the stuff he was doing. But we still argued a lot, though in a friendly way. I realized Newf had a big hand in the way the record was going to sound. When Kevin gave me that artwork and it said, "Produced by David Newfeld," I took a deep breath and said, "Yeah, it was."

KEVIN DREW_ Newf was like no other. No one in our circle was making sounds like him. No one was doing his production style. *You Forgot It In People* will always stand the test of time and be unique because it was made without any guidelines or any rules. Newf didn't know anything at the time; he didn't know what was cool and what wasn't. All he knew was music. He was a contemporary-pop-music junkie — he knew who Justin Timberlake and Avril Lavigne were because he went and did these weddings, and while we were in the middle of recording songs that would reference Stereolab and Pavement, he would be pulling out the *Hair* soundtrack! He had no idea about anything [happening in indie-rock], but he knew what great music was.

IT WAS MORE LIKE A RECORDING PROJECT THAT TURNED INTO A RECORD. BROKEN SOCIAL SCENE WAS STILL VERY MUCH AN IDEA AT THAT POINT.

BILL PRIDDLE_ I always call myself a founding non-member of Broken Social Scene. If I hadn't been in Treble Charger, maybe there would've been no [need for] Whitey [to join], and Kevin and

Brendan would just have me on lead guitar. But around the time when it made a lot more sense to do indie-rock, I was off trying to be a big major-label star. I really didn't want to make the last Treble Charger record [*Detox*], but we were on Nettwerk Management, and our previous record, *Wide Awake Bored*, had done really well. I had basically given up on the fact of being big in the U.S. and making millions of dollars, but still I was looking at Matthew Good and Our Lady Peace and thinking, "All we have to do is have the next record be a little bigger and get to that level and do a Canadian hockey-arena tour, and it's going to be $200,000 in my pocket and I'll buy a house in Toronto and I'll be set."

It was not fun at all making that last Treble Charger record. We were at Signal to Noise on Spadina and Adelaide, and I would finish up there at like 12:30 a.m. and go around the corner to Stars and Sons. I remember those guys were working on the feedback part in the song "Stars and Sons," and thinking, "You guys are so lucky — you get to do anything you want." But at the same time I thought, "At the end of the day, Treble Charger's record is going to sell 300,000 copies, and yours is going to sell 3,000 copies." And, of course, in the end our record sold about 60,000 to 80,000 copies and *You Forgot It In People* sold about 200,000 copies.

NOAH MINTZ_ Mastering usually takes one day, but there are a few albums I'll spend weeks on, and Broken Social Scene is always one of those albums. They just kept coming in and coming in — they were going crazy with revisions. I remember, by the tenth revision, Kevin gave me $200, and I said, "Dude, you don't have to give me money. Don't worry about it now." He said to me, "My grandma gave me this today for my birthday, and I have to give this to you — you've done so much work." So he gave me his birthday money.

JUSTIN PEROFF_ I remember taking the early recordings of [*You Forgot It In People*] to the Clear Spot, because I wanted to hear the tracks on a real sound system. Wednesdays were really dead — it was just Chris Harper behind the bar and myself. When it came to "Shampoo Suicide," I thought, "This mix is retarded. What is this?" Later, Kevin sat me down on his couch — there was always something about his living room: that stereo, the vibe — and we listened to the whole record from start to finish. And I said, "Kevin, this is a five-star record."

KEVIN DREW[3]_ Brendan Canning taught me how to end songs. When we made *Feel Good Lost*, I thought every song could've been ten minutes long. The whole ideology of trying to write a four-minute pop song was completely new to so many of us that we had so much fun doing it. We had already made our art-house albums. We worked in reverse: people usually make their records and then start to figure out sound. We all come from an understanding of sound; now we're trying to translate that understanding into the pop world. That exercise was completely intriguing and exciting to us. I would really love it when people would say, "They sound like Blue Rodeo and Yo La Tengo and Spiritualized and Cocteau Twins and Elton John and Earth, Wind & Fire." We didn't know how the album was going to go down; we actually thought we [had] made a compilation and not a record. I was scared to see if people were going to embrace the idea of a whole shitload of sounds on one album.

NOAH MINTZ_ "Collective" is an overused word, but it really defines a type of music: it's not just a couple of people's ideas. *You Forgot It In People* was a big collaborative effort that gelled into one piece.

BILL PRIDDLE_ I remember being at an early show with Kevin's dad [David Drew], and he said to me, "Bill, is Kevin ever going to make any money doing this?" And I said, "David, with this kind of music, Kevin isn't going to make a dime." But when I got *You Forgot It In People*, I just thought, "Holy shit." I remember being on tour with Treble Charger and telling everyone I knew, "Broken Social Scene, Kevin Drew — trust me, he's going to be the biggest thing in Canadian indie-rock in six months."

KEVIN DREW[4]_ I am not a great musician, as far as chops go — don't throw me in a room with a jazz musician. Priddle used the analogy that I was the glue — that is my role. I can say that as much as I can say Justin plays the drums. Brendan can play everything, basically; he can play the bass, he could put out a solo record of piano compositions. But the one thing that's happened is we've really established that Andrew Whiteman, Justin Peroff, Charles Spearin, Brendan, and myself are the core members of Broken Social Scene now. Attention has been directed toward me and Brendan because of the past, but it has to be stressed that those are the core members. Charlie is here 100 percent, but he's with Do Make Say Think, so when he's gone, the four of us are standing. And there's no way we couldn't say Dave Newfeld's a member. He is as much a member as Evan Cranley and James and Emily and Feist — even more so.

JOHN CROSSINGHAM_ I was a full-fledged member for *You Forgot It In People* — I have parts on at least eight of the thirteen songs. And then I left the band late that summer when the record was finished, which in some ways I never really recovered from. I don't think I was ever the same kind of full member in the band — even if I was internally, I wasn't externally. That's something I wrestled with for a long time.

ANDREW WHITEMAN_ I remember when Crossingham quit, but the joke is you can't quit. It's like the Cosa Nostra: "You in it, you can't get out." You either show up or you don't. Quitting is an unnecessary dramatic act, and there's enough of that.

JOHN CROSSINGHAM_ The reason I quit was my wife, Lesa, was nervous about me going away. I was never gone for more than a weekend to play shows. Raising the Fawn was starting to pick up a good head of steam, so Lesa was faced with her boy going away and touring with not just one but two bands. And Broken Social Scene needed an answer, like, "What kind of commitment can you give us?" In hindsight it was more like, "You didn't have to say you had to leave. You could've just said, 'I can't do this tour right now.'" But I wasn't used to bands working that way. I felt if I said, "I just can't do this right now," they would say, "What the fuck do you think this is, some kind of choose-when-you-want-be-in-this band?" What band works that way? Aside from Broken Social Scene, no one. I wasn't going to leave Raising the Fawn, so I quit Broken and said to Lesa, "Hey, babe, [their relationship] is what's most important." And I still feel that way: my relationship with my wife is what takes precedence over everything. But then *You Forgot It In People* became the biggest thing since sliced bread.

BUT THE ONE THING THAT'S HAPPENED IS WE'VE REALLY ESTABLISHED THAT ANDREW WHITEMAN, JUSTIN PEROFF, CHARLES SPEARIN, BRENDAN, AND MYSELF ARE THE CORE MEMBERS OF BROKEN SOCIAL SCENE NOW.

EVAN CRANLEY_ Stars were recording [their second album] *Heart*. We moved up to Montreal after living in Williamsburg, Brooklyn, for a while. I convinced everyone to move because it was so cheap to live there six years ago, and it just made so much sense: I was paying $100 in rent and we could have a little studio. I was doing *Heart* at the same time

MAJOR LABEL DEBUT

You Forgot It In People came out. That was a crazy time for me, because I was flip-flopping between both bands. It was exhausting, but I wasn't complaining — it was amazing.

JASON COLLETT_ The first record [*Feel Good Lost*] was being made when I was doing Radio Monday, and all those guys came and played [the night]: Whitey played it, Millan played it, Haines and Jimmy played it, Kevin played it. I wasn't interested in joining the band at that time because I had my hands full with the family and I was trying to get my own record together. When they were planning their first tour [for *You Forgot It In People*], they had asked me to open for them. They would back me up and then I would play in the band. That tour fell through, but I had way too much fun during the rehearsal.

I come from more of a traditional songwriting background, but I'm always so impressed how [in Broken Social Scene] songwriting is turned on its head. I think a big influence on that process has always been the Do Makes. Originally, Broken Social Scene was just an instrumental thing, and then when vocals were introduced, they were really treated as just another instrument, with stream-of-consciousness lyrics. Lyrics can really be cumbersome, and what's so great about the band is they never let them get in the way. There's an emotive level to what Kevin does that transcends any literal sense. People can relate to the songs on an instinctual, gut level — it's a higher form of communicating, really.

JULIE PENNER_ I had played Jason Collett's CD release show in November 2002, and after that, Kevin started leaving his classic long, rambling mes-

> I COME FROM MORE OF A TRADITIONAL SONGWRITING BACKGROUND, BUT I'M ALWAYS SO IMPRESSED HOW [IN BROKEN SOCIAL SCENE] SONGWRITING IS TURNED ON ITS HEAD.

sages on my answering machine. At first I didn't know what to make of them. I remember thinking, "Is this guy nuts?" At some point he asked me to play violin for the *You Forgot It In People* CD release at Lula Lounge. I had one practice session with the boys, which was all I needed.

AMY MILLAN_ My first show with Broken Social Scene was at the *You Forgot It In People* CD release party at Lula Lounge. Emily was in L.A., and Feist had moved to Paris. The girls were gone, so Kevin came to me and said, "I need you to be the girl." I was nervous because I knew I was around some incredible musicians, like Charles Spearin and Brendan Canning. I didn't really know the rest of the band as well as I knew Kevin. I had been singing with Emily since I was fifteen, so pulling off the Emily parts wasn't as difficult as [Feist's on] "Almost Crimes," which was a completely different way of singing for me — that firecracker Feist way. It was a really great show, and there was a definite atmosphere of excitement for something new that was going to be big. Then I ended up touring with the group for three years.

K-OS_ I saw Broken Social Scene at Lula Lounge. I don't know if he remembers this, but Kevin and I talked on the phone that week and he told me to come by and, if I felt like it, to join in. I was aware of no buzz, just the music and the audacity of having so many people onstage — you know, the whole Wu-Tang Clan comparison. I kept looking for a place to jump in or do some vocals, but [the show's momentum] was building by itself. I guess it was mostly the music's ultramagnetics that got me, and the nostalgia, which emanated from my high-school years. Everyone in that band reminded me of a close friend in high school that I had lost touch with. That's what appealed to me — the distant familiarity.

DANKO JONES_ There was one tour in particular that I came back home from and Brendan was on the cover of *Eye Weekly*, and I was like, "What the hell's going on?" Broken Social Scene had just kind of exploded. Every time we'd come home from Europe — we'd be out there for two months at a time — the only thing I really noticed was that Broken Social Scene's profile was getting bigger and bigger.

KEVIN DREW[5]_ When I talked to Lorraine Carpenter of the Montreal *Mirror*, she said, "Toronto is just viewed as a major-label town, but now we see that there are all these great bands coming out." There are all these great bands coming out because the indies are now putting out better music than the majors, and that's the way it's been for the past three years. There are more records coming out now from people involved in this record — my goal is to see a tree in some rock magazine, of who plays with who, showing all these people who lived within thirty-two blocks of each other and all their albums. The music in this town right now is not great — it's wonderful.

Flyer promoting the release of *You Forgot It In*

ARTS & CRAFTS
OPENS FOR BUSINESS

THE FIRST 1,000 COPIES of *You Forgot It In People* featured two record-label logos on their back cover: Paperbag Records, a new, upstart Toronto indie label that helped finance the initial run, and Broken Social Scene's own Arts & Crafts imprint, which at the time was a label in logo form only.

Arts & Crafts was the brainchild of Jeffrey Remedios, who in six years had risen through the ranks at Virgin Music Canada from co-op student intern in 1996 to the company's director of national publicity in 2002. A friend of Canning from the after-hours-party DJ days, Remedios also took in Drew as a roommate for six months in the fall of 2000. Remedios's immersion in the Broken Social Scene network, combined with his growing disillusionment with the quick-hit-or-pink-slip major-label culture, inspired him to approach Drew and Canning with the Arts & Crafts concept: part record company, part management team, part not-for-profit music community support system. The partnership with Paperbag Records was thus consistent with Remedios's initial vision of small local co-operatives pooling their resources for a common good.

But when *You Forgot It In People* started flying off the shelves of Rotate This and Soundscapes, Drew and Remedios quickly realized that their idealistic community-focused vision would have to take a backseat to the more practical matter of managing Broken Social Scene's burgeoning business, and they had to come to terms with the realization that their album had the potential to transcend the very community Arts & Crafts initially sought to support. Upon selling the first 1,000 copies of *You Forgot It In People*, Broken Social Scene parted ways with

Paperbag to facilitate Arts & Crafts' transformation into a self-sufficient, globally minded record label. (To assuage any hard feelings upon BSS's departure, Drew temporarily served as Paperbag's armchair A&R scout, bringing to the label, among others, his friends Stars — though they too eventually followed BSS to Arts & Crafts.)

Securing Canadian distribution for Arts & Crafts was a no-brainer. All Remedios had to do was knock on the door of his old EMI bosses, who offered not only distribution but office space as well. (Remedios's first recruit was another EMI exile, Daniel Cutler.) But Arts & Crafts' first real coup was scoring U.S. licensing through New York–based indie distribution empire Caroline. Initially the success of *You Forgot It In People* helped leverage releases like the BSS B-sides collection *Bee Hives*, a re-release of *Feel Good Lost*, Jason Collett's *Motor Motel Love Songs* (a reissue of his 2002 self-released album), the debut from Brendan Canning's chamber-rock side project Valley of the Giants (a collaboration with guitarist Anthony Seck and Godspeed You! Black Emperor's Sophie Trudeau), and Andrew Whiteman's Apostle of Hustle debut, *Folkloric Feel*. However, not all BSS affiliates were eager to join the new family business. Metric — who by late 2002 were in the process of scrapping their lustrous debut album, *Grow Up and Blow Away*, upon the collapse of their label, Restless Records — opted to sign with their lawyer Chris Taylor's new Toronto-based Last Gang imprint and emergent L.A.-based indie label Enjoy/Everloving Records.

But it was the platinum success of Feist's 2004 album, *Let It Die*, that effectively allowed Arts & Crafts to transcend the status of BSS boutique label. Today, the company employs twelve people (including at one point Drew's father, David, as Broken Social Scene's business manager) and is located in a chic downtown Toronto loft space.

The roster has expanded outside the immediate BSS community to include Australian chanteuse New Buffalo and Welsh indie-pop punters Los Campesinos! Parallel to the label's ascent has been the formation of the Experimental Parachute Moment, a filmmaking collective headed by Drew, Seck, and director George Vale that oversees video production for many Arts & Crafts artists.

It's a bit simplistic to call Arts & Crafts an indie label — if anything, it's a post-indie label, using both underground-schooled street smarts and major-label mechanisms to its advantage. Drew's involvement ensures that the artists' wishes and whims are respected and their careers are built gradually, while Remedios's industry connections have allowed Arts & Crafts to take advantage of the one thing major labels are still good at: shipping mass quantities of records to big chain stores across vast geographical expanses.

True to Remedios's original multidisciplinary vision, Arts & Crafts was also an early adopter of "360-degree" artist contracts, a novel but sometimes complicated arrangement wherein labels serve their artists not just through distribution, but also through management, merchandising, and publishing. The last has become an increasingly important revenue stream since indie musicians have become less reluctant to hear their songs used in commercials. Old-school indie-rock ideology demands an oppositional relationship between music and commerce, but Arts & Crafts' greatest feat has been to blur the distinction between which is the art and which is the craft.

Arts & Crafts logo. (JPF)

Back-cover art of Broken Social Scene's *You Forgot It In People.* (JPF)

Back-cover art for the 2003 UK edition of the seven-inch-single of "Stars and Sons." (JPF)

*JOE ENGLISH_* I had heard a couple of the *You Forgot It In People* demo tracks at Kevin's, and liked them. I remember saying one of the tracks reminded me of New Order. I don't think Kevin wanted to put the album out with Noise Factory, and I don't think I wanted to put it out, so we were at the same place at the same time. I don't think I could've put the record out the way he wanted it to be put out, just from a financial standpoint. Eventually they went the right way. No hard feelings — we started selling tons of *Feel Good Lost*. Before *You Forgot It In People*, the album sold maybe 500 copies; afterward, it sold between 5,000 and 10,000 copies. And that's just in Canada. Arts & Crafts sold another 12,000 to 15,000 worldwide.

*JEFFREY REMEDIOS_* I wanted to be paid to think, and I had pretty strong ideas on how [this label concept] should go. I knew that it had to begin and end with an act, and through karma and kismet and Brendan Canning, I ended up getting to know Kevin. Our first conversation was an indie-versus-major-label argument.

*KEVIN DREW_* Jeffrey had a lot of passion and a lot of knowledge that you can't find in [most] people. I wanted nothing to do with the record industry until I met him. And that's it — once you like someone, you like someone; it doesn't matter what they're doing. So I don't have the angst I had a couple of years ago.

*JEFFREY REMEDIOS_* My first conversation with Kevin and Brendan about a label was, "I have this idea. I want to call it Arts & Crafts; we want to band together under a name, but we won't be anything but a support resource on every level. We may be not-for-profit, but we'll just try to tie it all together to build this community up." We said from day one, "Let's go find a record label to help us out," because we didn't want to just be a label. That's why we brought Paperbag Records in to release *You Forgot It In People*. But the relationship was kind of flawed from the start, because it was Paperbag's first-ever release and they wanted to make their mark on the world; it was never going to work as a not-for-profit venture.

So before the first 1,000 copies were sold, Paperbag, Kevin, and I realized we needed to commercialize this [album release] on some level and maybe drill [Arts & Crafts' focus] down to music, because that's really what we know about. We can try to be a support system for the larger music community, but it was a bit naïve of us to think we could start with a macro approach. So we said, "Let's focus on the music, but then let's look at music in different ways." Let's take a 360-degree viewpoint — we said that from day one.

*KEVIN DREW_* The only reason I wanted to have this label was so that I could say no and "You can't pull any label bullshit on me because I own it!" Jeffrey wanted out of his job. I could tell he was one of those guys who wanted to run his own ship; I could tell he wanted to try to do something on his own. When he heard *You Forgot It In People* and he saw where we were going with it, it started to really piss him off, because he knew that we could do more with the album [than just release it locally]. He wanted to see this record do better than what was available for us in this country.

> *THE ONLY REASON I WANTED TO HAVE THIS LABEL WAS SO THAT I COULD SAY NO AND "YOU CAN'T PULL ANY LABEL BULLSHIT ON ME BECAUSE I OWN IT!"*

*LESLIE FEIST_* Kevin's role in Arts & Crafts is like the keeper of the flame. He's involved in the day-to-day in a very loose way, mostly in an A&R capacity — he makes amazing videos, he hears great bands, and he helps decide who to put out.

*JEFFREY REMEDIOS_* When I went to my employer [Virgin/EMI] and said, "I have this idea — and I'm leaving," they were really great. They said, "That sucks for us. How can we be involved?" The majors have realized they're going to have to outsource A&R and get into the distribution game. EMI gave us a distribution deal right away, so when I quit my job, I just moved down the hall.

We had to start in the U.S. and not do what the Canadian majors were doing — building a band in Canada and then exporting them abroad. Why not just export the albums and the artists ourselves? We could call the *Village Voice* just as easily as we could call *Eye Weekly*. There are thirty million people situated within a ten-hour drive of Toronto; twenty-five million of them live across the border. It made no sense for us to work east to west; it was more about working in concentric circles. We did that immediately. I did my Canadian distribution deal with EMI in December 2002 and I did my U.S. distribution deal in February 2003. It was really quick.

> *IT'S ALL ABOUT THE IDEA OF CREATING YOUR OWN WORLD, MAKING YOUR OWN MOM-AND-POP SHOP.*

*LESLIE FEIST_* It's all about the idea of creating your own world, making your own mom-and-pop shop. In 2003 I signed to Polydor France worldwide, and the deal-breaker for me was, "You've got to cut Canada out of the contract. I need to be on Arts & Crafts." I remember Jeff, Kevin, and I went to Utopia Café for a meeting, and part of me thought, "This is crazy — Kevin running a record label?" What I didn't realize was that Kevin came to the meeting to say to Jeff, "Never talk to me about this. I don't want to have anything to do with this project. This is my friend, and I don't want to get mixed up in the bullshit. I'm a silent partner on this one because I don't want to have her and I tripping over each other for the wrong reasons." So I

thought, "This is great! I get to be on your label but we don't have to ever talk about it!"

*JEFFREY REMEDIOS_* It's unclear if Feist's other label partners really knew what they had when they signed her. Leslie was amazing because she forced their hand and said, "You must give me Canada so I can put it out on Arts & Crafts," and they said, "Okay, we'll let your friends do this for you in Canada. Whatever." So when we outperformed every other territory for *Let It Die* — we were the only territory where she went platinum — we really shook up the system. They all took notice and started to look at our approach. We were also generating a ton of her content from here — videos, EPKs [electronic press kits]. We have to manoeuvre our way through this big system, but the irony of it is that I'm using all the skills that I developed during my time at Virgin.

*EMILY HAINES_* I remember that one of the biggest forks in the road that I've ever experienced was when Metric was in L.A. and we were going to leave [in 2003]. Right when we were going to leave, we got offered this deal to have Mike Andrews produce our next album for Enjoy Records. It was literally the day that Arts & Crafts were starting, and there was this whole question of whether to be on Arts & Crafts or not. I remember talking to Jeffrey and just being like, "Fuck, I don't know what to do . . ." George Vale made a really amazing Broken Social Scene EPK that had all these black-and-white photographs of everybody. Jeffrey and Kevin captured [what was special about the band]. I remember getting sent that EPK in L.A. and thinking, "Oh my god, this is so intense, I can't believe we're not a part of that." But the deciding factor was a really candid conversation James and I had about how the friendships were too fucking important. It's too risky. Sonically, Metric were becoming a little more wiry and a little more punk than the stuff that

Jeffrey Remedios and Brendan Canning in Austin, Texas, 2003. (JPF)

WE'VE BEEN EVANGELICAL IN THIS CONCEPT THAT SUCCESS AND FAILURE NEED TO BE JUDGED BY THE SIZE OF THE BUSINESS UNIT OF THE BAND.

was being released on Arts & Crafts. So the ultimate decision was, "We're already part of [the family]. We just don't need to have our purse strings tied to it." I can't be looking to Kevin to pay my royalty cheques.

BRENDAN CANNING_ I'm in a funny situation: I play in a band with a guy who owns half the label, and my manager [Jeffrey Remedios] owns the other half of the label. So I'm kind of fucked.

JEFFREY REMEDIOS_ It's a challenge. Your label's never been your management, traditionally. It's such a conflict, but artists are a big part of educating that the arrangement can work. If you build your deals transparently and truly make your decisions together, then it'll work.

KEVIN DREW[1]_ My father, once he stepped in and started to become the financial manager/organizer of all things Social Scene, would always look at me and say, "I don't know how you do this. Now you have to put on your schizophrenic hats" because I'll be in Social Scene talking about how the label has messed up and now we have to audit the label; at the same time, I am the label! And then Jeffrey's our manager and our label owner and my boss, but at the same time we're co-owners of the label. He runs the show; he's totally the head *capitan*. I'm almost the comic relief there at times. There are so many grey areas that have turned into pools. But you just swim . . . I don't know the temperature and I don't know how hot it is outside.

JEFFREY REMEDIOS[2]_ We've been evangelical in this concept that success and failure need to be judged by the size of the business unit of the band. That's all income and all expenses from touring, from licensing, from writing independently for commercials, from merchandising, and then also from record sales and from remixes and live-recording

sales. We don't talk about the number of records we sell by Apostle of Hustle; we talk about the business unit of Apostle of Hustle. We have a monthly score sheet that tells you exactly where the business unit is sitting. The record is one little beginning point.

EVAN CRANLEY_ Before Arts & Crafts, there were labels that ghettoized you and turned you into this non-stop touring machine where you played Kitchener, Ontario, eight times a year. They were obsessed with pumping their own product into their own backyard. Broken Social Scene and Arts & Crafts changed the Canadian musical landscape forever.

ALL MY FRIENDS IN MAGA- ZINES

TORONTO INDIE-ROCK
GOES GLOBAL

"THIS ONE'S FOR YOUR PIECE-OF-SHIT PRESIDENT." That's how Kevin Drew introduced "Cause = Time" at Broken Social Scene's South by Southwest showcase at Austin pub Momo's, on March 15, 2003, four days before the bombs fell on Baghdad. Given indie-rock fans' traditionally liberal disposition, the comment elicited mostly cheers from the capacity-defying crowd of 300, most of whom knew little about the band. *You Forgot It In People*'s official U.S. release was still months away, but a rave review from popular online magazine *Pitchfork* had piqued the interest of stateside indie enthusiasts, many of whom acquired the album through peer-to-peer download networks. (Among those in attendance was one of the band's heroes: Scott "Spiral Stairs" Kannberg of '90s indie-rock royalty Pavement and later Preston School of Industry.)

There is little that is overtly political in the music of Broken Social Scene, but in the early months of 2003, it seemed as if all the hope and fear infused in the band's music was playing out in newspaper headlines. While the Iraq War began the first chapter of its inevitably doomed script, closer to home, Toronto was dealing with its own crisis: a SARS outbreak had the international press portraying Toronto as a disease-infested quarantine zone, throwing the city's lucrative tourism industry into peril. And yet, given that Canada's national identity has been historically defined by the inability to define one, 2003 also marked the first time Canadians could not only assert a genuine ideological distinction from our neighbours to the south, but could do so from a position of confidence.

It was the year Prime Minister Jean Chrétien's Liberal government not only refused to support the dubious U.S. invasion of Iraq but also introduced bills to legalize gay marriage and decriminalize marijuana. Soon enough the Internet was teeming with sites like www.marryanamerican.ca, wherein disillusioned American liberals could seek love, matrimony, and, most important, Canadian citizenship. (Prime Minister Stephen Harper's Conservative government would bury the marijuana bill upon taking office in 2006, but, hey, it was fun while it lasted.)

In Toronto, a culture of civic appreciation emerged. New city-centric initiatives were appearing at the grassroots level, from *Spacing* magazine, a tri-annual publication devoted to analysis of public-space issues, to the Blocks Recording Club, a cooperative founded by former Hidden Cameras bassist Steven Kado, which gained renown for its unique handmade packaging, eclectic roster, and all-day veggie-potluck concerts. (Kado is also popularly credited with coining the term that would come to symbolize this new urban-enthusiast mindset: Torontopia.)

In the November 2003 issue of *GQ* magazine, a photo of Broken Social Scene appeared under the headline "Is Canada Cooler Than Us?"

The accompanying article suggested that Canada's progressive politics were a reflection of the collectivist music coming out of the country. The Hidden Cameras, Constantines, and Royal City had all signed international deals with esteemed indie labels like London's Rough Trade and Seattle's Sub Pop, while Broken Social Scene marked the year by winning a Juno award for Best Alternative Album, signing a major-label deal in the U.K. with Mercury Records affiliate Vertigo (to coincide with their first overseas shows at London's Barfly and the Route du Rock Festival in St. Malo, France), and selling out two homecoming shows at Toronto's 1,200-capacity Phoenix Concert Theatre.

By the end of the year, the media attention bestowed upon Broken Social Scene had begun to spill over to its subsidiaries, including Feist (who was already becoming a star in her own right in France), Jason Collett, Stars, Do Make Say Think, Apostle of Hustle, Raising the Fawn, and Metric, who released their breakthrough album, *Old World Underground, Where Are You Now?* The question posed by that title would ultimately prove to be moot: the underground was now everywhere.

But if 2003 saw Broken Social Scene touring for the experience and excitement, 2004 was the year they began touring for a living, enlisting a full-time soundman, Marty Kinack, and European tour manager, Nadin Brendel. In North America, the band's popularity continued to surge. At their return visit to South by Southwest in March 2004, Broken Social Scene played to over 2,000 people at outdoor venue Stubb's, where the opening riffs to "KC Accidental" and "Stars and Sons" were greeted with instant roars of recognition. In May they performed at the Coachella Festival in Indio, California (where a reinstituted John Crossingham proposed to his girlfriend, Lesa, onstage), and that summer they joined Canadian indie-rock patriarchs Sloan and emergent Montreal ensemble Arcade Fire for an all-day concert on Toronto's Olympic Island; the event's success inspired Broken Social Scene to stage their own curated festival on the island the following two summers.

But the concentrated markets in Europe proved to be more of a challenge. While BSS became fixtures on the summer festival circuit — introducing them to fans-turned-friends like Bloc Party — success was elusive in the U.K., where the image-obsessed music press saw little pin-up potential in an unwieldy gang of well-bearded Canadians. The *NME* review for the "Stars and Sons" single even went so far as to say BSS looked like a bunch of kiddie-porn collectors — and that was one of the positive write-ups. (The band would eventually negotiate out of their U.K. deal with Mercury, opting to release their records overseas through Arts & Crafts.)

Broken Social Scene's August 27 headline appearance at Toronto's Harbourfront Centre saw the outdoor amphitheatre swarming with 4,000 fans, though many in the crowd were unsure whether they were welcoming the band back or bidding them farewell — just a few days earlier, Kevin Drew had announced that it would be Broken Social Scene's last show, a statement reiterated in that week's *NOW* magazine cover story. Of course, it was bullshit. But the simple PR prank hinted that life on the road was not all group hugs and handclaps.

Left to right: Leslie Feist, Andrew Whiteman, Kevin Drew, Jason Collett, and Brendan Canning (*top*); Kevin Drew, Jason Collett, Leslie Feist, Brendan Canning, Andrew Whiteman, and Justin Peroff (*bottom*) in Austin, Texas, for South by Southwest, 2003. (JPF)

DAVE BOOKMAN_ Let's give credit where credit is due: *Pitchfork* made BSS in the U.S. They were like the original MySpace/Facebook. The site is like a virtual indie record store.

JEFFREY REMEDIOS_ In hindsight, I think any number of things would've catapulted *You Forgot It In People* forward. It was already really happening here, and the distribution deal with Caroline was already done in the U.S. Things were taking a natural momentum, but *Pitchfork* really made it go farther faster. At the band's first show in New York, at Other Music, there was a lineup around the corner.

JUSTIN PEROFF_ After playing South by Southwest, I thought, "Okay, there are people here from Spain coming up to me, asking if we're signed," and The Stills, who we played with, were telling us they were fans. After that I thought, "I really think this is happening — there are people lining up around the corner for us in Texas."

CHARLES SPEARIN_ There were all these touring invitations after that record came out. Do Make Say Think was still a big priority, and *Winter Hymn Country Hymn Secret Hymn* was being recorded then, so I turned down the Broken Social Scene tour that basically turned the band into a real band. They did South by Southwest, which is famous now — at least from what I've heard many times — for how great it was. That was when the band came together. I got married, Kevin was always waiting for me to get back from tour or a retreat, and he clearly had had enough of that, and was like, "I have to be able to tour without you." So they got Jason Collett in.

ANDREW WHITEMAN_ Jason Collett — his influence and aura — was so important. He came in because Charles couldn't tour, and he had the van and he was there for those big moments. His big-brothery calmness was key.

JASON COLLETT_ When we started touring, the thing that blew me away was that people were coming from such great distances to see the show. People were travelling from a state or two away, and they might be underage and risk not getting in. Some of them didn't — they stood outside on the street, just to be close to something. That brought back all the stuff that, as a kid, was so important to me and that cut through the shitty suburb where I grew up — music was like a lifeline. At our first shitty little show in Camden Town in London, a couple of girls had travelled twenty-four hours from Poland to be there. There was no record out in Europe yet, but the clubs were full. There was something vital about the spirit of the music that people related to on the ground level.

ANDREW WHITEMAN_ We went across the U.S. with Stars in Collett's van, and then we signed this stupid deal with Mercury Records in the U.K. I was like, "I got a chunk of change — holy shit, I can quit my job and do this all the time."

JASON COLLETT — HIS INFLUENCE AND AURA — WAS SO IMPORTANT. HE CAME IN BECAUSE CHARLES COULDN'T TOUR, AND HE HAD THE VAN AND HE WAS THERE FOR THOSE BIG MOMENTS.

JO-ANN GOLDSMITH_ I remember when Broken Social Scene won the Juno for the first time, sitting in the chair with Kevin, holding hands, being so afraid that they were going to win or weren't going to win. I mean, it's just the Junos, but it was also a moment, like, "Oh my god, we weren't even going for that." We were just making music to play it, and all of a sudden we're thrown into this crazy business. After the Junos, Jason Collett and Justin and myself and Brendan had a huge pillow fight. They were very romantic, exciting, innocent times.

AMY MILLAN_ Stars and Broken toured together across Canada, and it became pretty clear by the end of it that *You Forgot It In People* was a really big record and affected people in a big way. It was hard to compete: there'd be five of us onstage in Stars and then sixteen of us onstage in Broken Social Scene. It was supposed to a be a split co-headlining bill, but by the end of it we agreed, "If we're all going to be in Broken, we might as well end it with Broken." It was interesting — I think we have very different fans. Stars has more dentists and hygienists and maybe nurses; we dip into the older, post-forty crowd. Stars will never be as hip as Broken Social Scene, but our fans are too old to know how to download records, so they'll actually buy them.

*JASON COLLETT_* We were at a point in music history where the industry was in such turmoil; it had been treating the whole change — because of the Internet — with such fear. By putting out shit records for so long that are overpriced and that might have one good song on them — that created a really cynical audience. So everybody started downloading, simply to have more access to better things, something real. Everything that the spirit of the band represented at the time had a certain romance and exhilaration and most of all, a certain lack of calculation. Because it started out in the basement, and it would've continued to happen in the basement, it just accidentally took off.

*EVAN CRANLEY_* *You Forgot It In People* spawned a lot of success for other bands, no doubt about it. Stars would've continued making records even if [*You Forgot It In People*'s success] didn't happen. But it was because of that record that we got a lot of residual press. There was a definite resurgence in indie music again, and we were definitely a part of that.

*JAMES SHAW_* It was going so well for everyone; it just seemed like Broken were leading the crew. It's like you have the Toronto Maple Leafs and you have

the Montreal Canadiens, and then you have Team Canada — it makes sense that Team Canada would be better. It felt good because I was a part of it; it also felt frustrating because I wanted the same success to happen to Metric, and it wasn't happening at first. *Old World Underground* never really took until after almost two years. It wasn't until when we decided to stop touring and make another record that all of a sudden we looked back and went, "Oh shit, it kind of went well . . . we sold almost 100,000 records." We didn't really see it happen because we were too busy playing.

*EVAN CRANLEY_* Touring with Social Scene was one of the easiest, most effortless, non-anxiety-filled times of my life, because with that band it just flowed so easily. It was one of the happiest times for me playing in a band ever. We'd sing "Looks Just Like the Sun" at some festival, and the sun would start poking through the clouds. It was like a fairy tale. There was so much love between everyone that it made it easy. There was no bullshit yet.

*MARTY KINACK_* Champ had been asking me to do sound for a year before I actually started, but I was recording Sarah Harmer's album at the time. For some reason the band respected me right off the bat, even though I had never heard *You Forgot It In People*. I don't have any of their albums. I might have one on vinyl because they accidentally left it at my house. I've never taken a set list because I still don't know the names of the songs.

*EMILY HAINES_* Metric and Broken Social Scene did just a few shows together, but I have really fond memories of playing Buffalo and places like that. I remember driving down the highway behind their van; we'd pass CDs back and forth through the windows, kind of like a *Footloose* thing. Kevin was so ridiculously a diva — he had no sense of owing anybody anything. He'd go onstage and be like, "I'm

Left to right: Andrew Whiteman, Brendan Canning, and Leslie Feist, playing in Camden, England, on the band's first European tour in August 2003. (LF)

FOR A LOT OF US, IT'S LIKE, "WOW, THIS IS EVERYTHING WE WANTED AND SO MUCH MORE!" AND THE NEXT THING YOU KNOW YOU'RE DRUNK FOR SIX MONTHS AND YOU FORGOT TO CALL YOUR MOTHER FOR THREE MONTHS OF THAT.

Kevin Drew, 2003. (JPF)

EVERYTHING THAT THE SPIRIT OF THE BAND REPRESENTED AT THE TIME HAD A CERTAIN ROMANCE AND EXHILARATION AND MOST OF ALL, A CERTAIN LACK OF CALCULATION.

Left to right: Justin Peroff, Amy Millan, and Evan Cranley on tour in Belgium, 2004. (JS)

broken social scene

*

death is a b-side

Original art from Broken Social Scene's *Bee Hives* album, 2004. (JPF)

Brendan Canning performs the classic gazing-out-the-tour-bus-window pose, 2003. (JPF)

Charles Spearin, 2003. (JPF)

not feeling this at all . . . Ladies and gentlemen, I don't want to be here!" In Broken, no one's willing to put their shit aside to play the show. If someone's got a crick in their neck, you're going to feel it when they play. If someone had a bad hummus plate backstage, it's going to affect the show.

TORQUIL CAMPBELL_ It's always been fun touring with Broken. They're a bunch of road warriors. It's not like it's their first band — they've all played Calgary fifteen times, other than Kevin. And that's the magic of it: you've got all these dudes around like Andrew and Jason and Brendan, who are very calm individuals and also very experienced, and Kevin's neither calm nor experienced. But they need that; they need his naïveté and his energy and his willingness to question why things are the way they are.

MARTY KINACK_ Everybody realized they were unbelievably lucky to be [touring]. You can't take it for granted; most people have to save up for a year to travel for a week overseas. Meanwhile, one day we're in Bilboa, we get on the bus, the next thing you know we're somewhere in France; two days later we're in Norway.

NADIN BRENDEL_ It might sound unbelievable, but Broken Social Scene came over [to Europe] and were embraced with sold-out shows from the very first date. I remember how the festival programmers of Roskilde [in Denmark] and Werchter [in Belgium] rushed out of their offices to see the band live, and how, upon settlement [payment], a lot of the promoters were still speechless. I don't know if the band ever broke even, but I think, even if they did, Kevin would probably just invite some more of his buddies to come along and play the seventh or eighth guitar.

GORDON MOAKES_ My first memory of seeing Broken Social Scene play was at the Accelerator Festival in Stockholm in 2004. Bloc Party were in the middle of making our first record in Copenhagen, so it was a short hop to go over and play this show. I went to watch BSS play, knowing they were going to clash with our set, hoping to catch a few songs. They played a huge chunk of *You Forgot It In People* and I was transfixed. I was mesmerized by Amy Millan and by Kevin. I literally couldn't tear myself away. Eventually our manager had to come and drag me backstage to play.

SCOTT KANNBERG_ I was playing some Preston School of Industry shows and there was an opportunity to play with Broken Social Scene in Atlanta [in April 2004], and that's where I met Kevin. He proceeded to get really, really smashed. I remember the rest of the band being kind of mad at us because they thought he got really wasted because of us. I felt really bad. Since then we've become friends. Kevin and I have a lot in common — our stories and our love of music — so we bonded that way. He's a very loving soul. The band is like one big group hug. It makes me look at myself and become a better person somehow.

MARTY KINACK_ I always felt a bit like the dad because I'm the oldest by far. Everybody in some form or another would come to me with their problems, some in way larger forms than I'd ever want. I'm not going to mention any names — ahem, Kevin Drew — but that made me feel really good, that people were coming to me for advice.

KEVIN DREW[1]_ I'm fortunate to have the Brendan Cannings and the Jason Colletts and the Marty Kinacks in our band: people who are standing solidly on their feet and not getting pushed by anything. For a lot of us, it's like, "Wow, this is everything we wanted and so much more!" And the next thing you know you're drunk for six months and you forgot to call your mother for three months of that.

KEN SOCI

EXT MANDANA TOWHIDY PHOTOGRA...

Time Out New York

MUSIC

Social insecurity

Broken Social Scene, Toronto's unwieldy alt-rock collective, tries to fit in with the big kids by Jem Aswad

THE VERGE

THE CULTURE WAR
//The Canada Conundrum//

NORTHERN NEIGHBORS MAKE US LOOK BAD

Is Canada Cooler Than Us?

* Canada's next great indie group: Broken Social Scene.

160 GQ NOVEMBER 2003

Photograph by **CHRISTOPHER WAHL**

Rolling Stone

New Faces

Broken Social Scene

The Toronto collective makes a shockingly fresh indie-rock album

It's not all boys in BSS. Some members are not pictured, including a couple of women. See who shows up when the group tours this sum...

With as many as sixteen members and song titles such as "I'm Still Your Fag," Toronto's Broken Social Scene have improbably produced one of the year's freshest indie-rock albums – the excellently out-there *You Forgot It in People*. Brimming over with symphonic clatter, subtle atmospherics and spacey pop melodies, *People* is what might result if a jazz orchestra wrote first-rate pop tunes and recorded them in a garage. It's a remarkable turnaround from the band's first album, 2001's *Feel Good Lost*, a mostly rambling, instrumental affair. "We played gigs for a year and didn't play anything from the record," says singer-guitarist Kevin Drew (*far right*). Though *People* contains shorter, more accessible material, the band's jamming jones is still present. Says Drew, "We were like, 'Is there room for harmonica? Sure, there's room for fuckin' harmonica!'" **CHRISTIAN HOARD**

RECORD REVIEWS

tchfork

...views
...ws
...tures
...kcast
...t New Music

[GO]

RSS Feed

Broken Social Scene
You Forgot It in People
[Arts & Crafts/Paper Bag; 2002]
Rating: 9.2
» Buy it from Amp Camp
» Download it from Emusic

It's a bit late to be talking about New Year's Resolutions, but mine was to dig through the boxes upon boxes of promos that arrive at the Pitchfork mailbox each month, and listen

Top and bottom row, left to right: Amy Millan, Marty Kinack, James Shaw, and Evan Cranley.
Second row, left to right: Brendan Canning, Andrew Whiteman, Justin Peroff, Jason Collett, and Kevin Drew.
Third row, left to right: Dave Hodge, Nadin Brendel, Jeffrey Remedios, and Charles Spearin. (JR)

MARTY KINACK_ In terms of partying, Broken goes to eleven. In some bands there might be one or two who are always ready to go. But in Broken you can always find a handful of people. Especially when we're on a bus — any other band, the party ends when the bus has to leave and you kick off all your friends and girls and stuff, but for us it's like, "All right, we've got twelve people, the bus is full, we're rolling down the highway, cranking the reggae!"

LESLIE FEIST_ I went back and forth [between Paris and Toronto] — I don't think I ever flew back just for a Broken tour, but if I was around I would do the shows. And I liked that I never had to ask. The fact that the notoriety was building on the external side hadn't changed the inside yet. It all stayed mellifluous. I always looked at it like this doughnut, like the centre was the constant five who held down the fort. Then when I'd come back, sometimes Crossingham would be there, sometimes not. Sometimes the horns would be there, sometimes there were no horns. Cranley, Amy, Emily, Shaw, Crossingham, and I would be the satellites. It's like a wild-west saloon, like on *Deadwood*: there's the proprietors working hard to keep it open, with the doors swinging and all these characters coming in and out all the time — it's like a watering hole for us. [Brendan and Kevin] kept it running, but we kept it in business.

AMY MILLAN_ The biggest danger with Broken Social Scene was that it would become a commercial of itself. What I remember about Broken Social Scene is that we never played the same show twice, and we often played behind a curtain with images on it — there would be no face — with huge, epic swelling tunes that didn't even have vocals. So that's the most important thing to remember: the band always has to reinvent itself.

BRENDAN CANNING_ It's a little less about artistic expression when it becomes a travelling road show. You have to program your performance like a play.

EVAN CRANLEY_ The impromptu magic that originally defined Broken Social Scene was kind of lost when it became more about putting on a show. I'd be in Stockholm with Stars, get on a plane and meet up with Broken, and we'd write out the set list. There couldn't be too many left turns because it would become impossible to get through a show. The shows became more regimented, but they were still fantastic. The notion of us playing at Ted's Wrecking Yard was lost. The band just evolved.

JUSTIN PEROFF_ I was making posters for our Harbourfront show [in August 2004], and Kevin said, "When you make this one, write THE LAST SHOW on it." I just rolled my eyes. It's funny, but it's like, "Come on, I'm not that guy; I don't want to mess with the fans." But Kevin's the Madonna/marketing genius of the band. Honestly, I think it's partly about playing with power. You're given a role because you manifested an audience and people are listening. You can say whatever you want, and people might believe it. If you say that we're breaking up . . . Well, did you see how many people were at that Harbourfront show? A lot of fucking people. In a way, it might be Kevin's way of gauging the fans' reaction.

THE BIGGEST DANGER WITH BROKEN SOCIAL SCENE WAS THAT IT WOULD BECOME A COMMERCIAL OF ITSELF.

JASON COLLETT_ I found it all very humorous because I knew the band was never breaking up. Everybody perhaps benefited and suffered from Kevin's various whims, and it's just part of the package. He's got an uncanny, savant-like instinct for songs, but also for the industry. I don't know how calculated any of it may have been to gather attention, but it's certainly served us well to announce various breakups on the way.

THE FIRST TWO BROKEN SOCIAL SCENE ALBUMS WERE BORN OUT OF LOVE — THEY WERE NEW RELATIONSHIPS FOR EVERYONE IN THE BAND, GETTING TO KNOW EACH OTHER, THROWN INTO THIS HOUSE WHERE THERE WAS ALWAYS GOOD EATING, THERE WERE ALWAYS PEOPLE AROUND, THERE WAS ALWAYS THIS ONGOING BEAUTIFUL PARTY THAT NEVER ENDED.

AMY MILLAN_ I think [the "last show"] is a frame of mind. It's how to look at every show you play, because it just might be the last. Kevin Drew's a bit of a fatalist. Try taking a plane with that guy — he's like, "We'll die legends!"

ANDREW WHITEMAN_ Everything Kevin does is his way of acting out. The glasses he puts on are like [those of] a comedic struggling teenager in an '80s movie. That's how he views the world — like a character in a John Hughes movie. The wonderful thing about his art is that he feels so entitled to things; he doesn't censor himself. And it also means that he loves the laundry — he loves to sing about the laundry.

EVAN CRANLEY_ There's always been this vibe about the band that it's all going to fall apart. Like [the song] "It's All Gonna Break." And that's what's great about it: you get some really good tension. Those tours in 2004 were incredibly blissful, but at the same time we were asking ourselves a lot of questions about where we were in our personal lives, and maybe we weren't the people that we'd thought we'd be, and maybe this life isn't forever.

TORQUIL CAMPBELL_ I've been in this business we call show all my life — doing movies [as a child actor], doing interviews, and travelling around, and flirting with the idea of notoriety. So when the success started to really happen with the bands, for me

it was just another go-round on this inevitable trip that proved to me how insignificant I was and how mortal we all are and how pointless life is. But other people in the band had never experienced that, and all their lives had been moving toward this moment of being heard. And then they were heard, and that's like an earthquake inside you — it fucks with your whole perception of everything.

JO-ANN GOLDSMITH_ The first two Broken Social Scene albums were born out of love — they were new relationships for everyone in the band, getting to know each other, thrown into this house where there was always good eating, there were always people around, there was always this ongoing beautiful party that never ended. There weren't a bunch of people around blowing smoke up your ass all the time — that's when things started to cave in for me. I started getting really unhappy that there were all these strangers around all the time. It got really intense because everyone just wanted a piece; they wanted to talk with you, drink with you, do drugs with you, party with you. I know that sounds contradictory, since it's supposed to be about this big collective. But it's hard to do that, to find the balance. Once money gets involved and people get involved and industry gets involved — the collective can't thrive in that environment, because everything starts getting picked apart and divided, and people want a piece of everything, and then people think maybe they should do their own thing. The collective collapses. It's inevitable in any situation, but it's also a very sad death, because that's what I loved — the collective mentality.

EMILY HAINES_ It was a difficult time for me: Jimmy and I had broken up, my father [poet Paul Haines] had died, and all I did was tour. I could not be on the road and afford to pay the rent, so I didn't have an apartment for a year. It really fucks with your head.

"Cause = Time" video, 2003. (GV)

Andrew Whiteman in the foreground performing with Broken Social Scene on their European festival circuit, 2004. (JR)

Poster promoting Broken Social Scene's "Final Show" at Harbourfront Centre in Toronto, 2004. (JPF)

We did that Harborfront show, and it was the first time I had seen all those guys because they had all gone to Europe and they all had these huge epiphanies: Amy and Evan got together, Kevin and Jo-Ann were breaking up; Jimmy and I had already broken up, so he had gone to Europe with [Broken Social Scene]. And I had started working on my solo record [*Knives Don't Have Your Back*], so that [Harbourfront show] was the first we had all been back together. And I remember doing rehearsals where we were all in a room standing in a circle, and it was cool. That's how I thought we should've made the next record, because it was so amazing. But because it was going to be produced by Dave [Newfeld], everything had to go through this weird portal, and everything became really fractured and refracted through a weird prism, a dark stone. I'm not criticizing Dave; it's just that that was a weird place for all of us to go to in order to get to each other.

*JUSTIN PEROFF_* We toured the world, and with that you become tangled up in your head, thinking, "What is this?" and "How come I can't remember 2003?" And there was some spicy romantic politics going on. When you throw sixteen people on a bus, including lovers, it's like, "Can you just turn away for a couple of seconds? I want some time alone." And there's a lot of drinking involved when you're getting free booze every night. And then of course there's the anticipation of the next record as well — you can't help but consider what everybody's going to think.

Ticket stub from Broken Social Scene's show at Barfly in Camden, England, August 12, 2003. (JPF)

IT'S ALL GONNA BREAK

THE UNMAKING OF BROKEN SOCIAL SCENE

ON OCTOBER 11, 2005 — almost three years to the date from the release of *You Forgot It In People* — Broken Social Scene issued their self-titled third album. Based on thirty-one critiques — ranging from a perfect score of one hundred from U.K. webzine *Playlouder* to a middling rating of fifty from the *New York Times* — review-aggregate website metacritic.com awards *Broken Social Scene* an average score of eighty-two, an indication that the band successfully lived up to the hype surrounding the record's long-awaited release. But if the album felt like less of a victory than the more universally praised *You Forgot It In People*, it's probably because Broken Social Scene were too exhausted to celebrate it.

Everything about the album, it seemed, was a source of tension and open to second-guessing: the piecemeal recording process (split between Stars and Sons and Ohad Benchetrit's home studio); producer Dave Newfeld's obsessive attention to detail and radical approach to mixing; the lengthy running time (sixty-six minutes, ten longer than *You Forgot It In People*); the oft-delayed release date (which put the record in the awkward position of competing against Metric's new album, *Live It Out*); not to mention the fact that the band's catchiest new song — a revved-up Strokes-like rocker called "Major Label Debut" — was reworked into a slow, hazy ballad for fear of seeming like an obvious bid for a pop single. Various celebrity guests — including k-os and Murray Lightburn of the Montreal art-rock sextet The Dears — were enlisted for vocal contributions, only to have their tracks mixed and mutated beyond recognition. The oblique liner-note scribbles underscore the air of confusion and restlessness: "forgive yourself," "write more songs about fear," "practice vocals between fights," "slice up your arm (if necessary)," and "blame the president for destroying our marriage." In the last example, the band weren't just being melodramatic: Kevin Drew and Jo-Ann Goldsmith separated during the album's recording.

The stress surrounding the album seemed to manifest itself in the infamous events of July 13, 2005, when Canning's roommate, George Vale, drove down to New York City with Newfeld to meet up with Broken Social Scene the night before a Central Park show with Dinosaur Jr. Vale went to buy some marijuana from a dealer on Lexington Avenue, with Newfeld tagging along. After Vale completed his purchase, he and Newfeld were surrounded by four undercover policemen. **Thinking they were muggers, Newfeld pushed one of the officers away; in return, he received several bruised ribs, two black eyes, a bloodied face — grisly photos of which were posted on *Pitchfork* — and a charge of resisting arrest.** Both spent the night in jail, and while Vale had his pot charge dropped — because the arresting officers were actually on a crack sting — Newfeld pleaded innocent to the charges of resisting arrest and possession of an illegal substance, both of which were eventually dropped. (On the counsel of a lawyer hired by the band, Newfeld later filed a civil suit against the City of New York and the arresting NYPD officer for "infringement of the constitutional right to be free of excessive force," and settled out of court for $60,000 in 2007.)

In spite of all this tumult — or perhaps in stubborn defiance of it — *Broken Social Scene* expresses its anxieties through ecstatic, often exhilarating gestures: the blissful brass finale of "Ibi Dreams of Pavement," the rousing Drew/Feist back-and-forth on "7/4 (Shoreline)," the breakbeat blitzkrieg of "Windsurfing Nation," the emotional roller-coaster momentum of "Superconnected," and the Boléro-like cavalry charge that provides the payoff to ten demanding minutes of "It's All Gonna Break." Though it was first written in 2001, the band was predestined to save the last song for release in 2005 — because that year it all very nearly did.

On the eve of *Broken Social Scene*'s release, Kevin Drew told me, "Sure, I'd like to go play on *Letterman*, but no music's going to change to get to that." It didn't — and Broken Social Scene got their date at the Ed Sullivan Theater anyway. The band's June 2006 *Letterman* appearance was just one highlight in a year that saw the band ticking off career milestones like items on a grocery list: another Best Alternative Album Juno award win; a *Late Night with Conan O'Brien* visit; a radio session in Australia with their hero-turned-friend Scott Kannberg; soundtrack work for the Alan Rickman/Sigourney Weaver film *Snow Cake* and Ryan Gosling's star-making *Half Nelson*; a benefit show in Toronto backing up Dinosaur Jr.'s J Mascis to raise money for Indian humanitarian Amma; another Olympic Island music festival appearance, this time with international representation from their Bloc Party mates; and a triumphant stand at Lollapalooza in Chicago's Grant Park, where a crowd of 20,000 demanded an encore for ten minutes after the set's end (only to be silenced by the sound of the headlining Red Hot Chili Peppers, playing across the field). And if *Broken Social Scene* had divided North American critics, the U.K. press — which had been cool toward *You Forgot It In People* — lavished the record with praise and hyperbole, with *Uncut* magazine awarding the album five stars in its February 2006 issue. That May the band sold out London's 1,500-capacity Koko Theatre.

However, achieving these milestones required a certain amount of logistical restructuring. Rather than trying to work around Feist's, Amy Millan's, and Emily Haines's increasingly busy schedules, Broken Social Scene hired a new female singer, Lisa Lobsinger (a fan they had met on tour in Calgary), to handle their parts in absentia, while violinist Julie Penner was brought into the fold full-time to fill out the sound (and possibly balance out a now estrogen-deficient lineup). And where the band once routinely used live shows to develop new material, the 2006 tours saw no new songs introduced to the set list; the band's ceaseless touring schedule and expanding fan base demanded that they stick to the tried-and-true crowd-pleasers. Whether it was out of exhaustion, a sense of satisfaction with all they had accomplished, or perhaps the changing backstage dynamic caused by Drew's year-long romance with Feist (formerly Andrew Whiteman's long-time on-again/off-again girlfriend), the band announced that their November 26, 2006, performance at Ann Arbor's Michigan Theater with Do Make Say Think would be their last show. Until the next one, of course.

DAVE NEWFELD_ After *You Forgot It In People*, everyone said, "We're going to need another album. We're going to do it with you. All systems go — let's keep this thing happening." And then the touring started, and the band had to be away for a long time. So we did the *Bee Hives* B-sides album because Mercury in the U.K. kept saying, "We need another B-side for this single." Then I did Whitey's Apostle of Hustle record [*Folkloric Feel*]; we spent about three months on that. There was a bunch of shit in the middle — we did the soundtrack for the Bruce McDonald film *The Love Crimes of Gillian Guess*. The momentum never stopped after *You Forgot It In People*. By early 2004 we were working on the self-titled album, right through to June 2005.

BRENDAN CANNING_ There was no solid focus throughout the recording of the third album. It wasn't like, "Hey, the band's going to make a record!" It was more like, "Okay, we're going to record a little bit . . . we're going away again . . . we're coming back." And we left it all up to Dave to wrangle the stuff.

CHARLES SPEARIN_ I had a kid, and Newfeld works from midnight to eight in the morning, which was great for *You Forgot It In People*, but I was trying to keep my shit together at home.

DAVE NEWFELD_ I can do good stuff in the daytime, but the night is best because you know the phone isn't going to ring. Everyone's gone to sleep, so all of a sudden all the pressure of other people's concerns has drifted away. It really frees your mind up. And you want that space sometimes where you can think clearly and no one's going to interrupt you. There are different parts of yourself being accessed when other people aren't around.

OHAD BENCHETRIT_ Newf is an erratic individual with an erratic schedule. [The two-studio set-up] would just be a way to give him his space. We would work with Newf when it was good to work with Newf, and when it wasn't, we could work at my place and not be stuck in limbo, doing nothing. You have to work within Newf's personality, so that means you're not always working when you want to work — that's the unfortunate part. Having two studios was the way of getting around that.

CHARLES SPEARIN_ I ended up being more of an observer for *Broken Social Scene* . . . "It's All Gonna Break" was written a long time ago, and I had a lot to do with writing it, but I didn't feel like I made 100,000 decisions on that album — I felt like I made 100 decisions. So I had to swallow my pride and listen to it and say, "It's a good record." And it is a good record; the songs are great. I was happy with it from a kind of outside perspective.

BRENDAN CANNING[1]_ Newf's a little more prominent on this record because we were away sometimes, and he would get things done. Part of the problem is being away and coming back and working on an album piecemeal — it takes a while to wrap your head around songs that have been worked on when you're not around. "Hotel" was originally supposed to be a remix for [the Feist song] "One Evening." It's strange: the birth of certain tracks on this record and where they ended up. The album is even more of a leap than *You Forgot It In People*, because some of these tracks started in one place and leapt into a whole other zone.

K-OS_ I don't remember whose idea it was [to do a song together] . . . I know that Kevin called me. There was a lot of love and respect there, and Kevin had brought up [the example of] A Tribe Called Quest, and that was all I needed to hear. I saw BSS at South by Southwest and they told me that the song we did ["Windsurfing Nation"] wasn't going to be on the album. Justin said he liked it, but

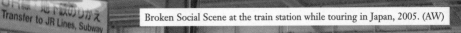

Broken Social Scene at the train station while touring in Japan, 2005. (AW)

THE ALBUM IS EVEN MORE OF A LEAP THAN *YOU FORGOT IT IN PEOPLE*, BECAUSE SOME OF THESE TRACKS STARTED IN ONE PLACE AND LEAPT INTO A WHOLE OTHER ZONE.

The crowd at a concert in Japan, 2006. (AW)

Andrew Whiteman onstage in Australia, 2006. (JP)

Scott Kannberg (formerly of Pavement) and Justin Peroff in Australia, 2006. (JPF)

Jason Collett and John Crossingham at Kool Haus in Toronto, 2006 (RV)

Brendan had doubts, so it was an on-again/off-again idea. Sometimes when musicians get together to make music it's like sex: there is so much potential in the idea, but at some point potential has to transmute into physical manifestation. Everything has to be fair and equal and balanced, and I was worried, I guess. BSS was becoming, or had become, such a huge idea, I didn't want to be overshadowed by that, or pose. That was my only hesitation, really — being the token, or the music sounding forced.

One summer day, Kevin picked me up in a rental car. He said, "I'm gonna play you the track but I'm gonna change things a little." With an intro like that, I kind of got butterflies, because either that was total bullshit and the song sucked or he really liked it. He put the song on, and from the intro I was all in: that door opening, with the sound of footsteps of someone walking in — that totally reflected how the track went down, because I literally came through the door at Newfeld's all spontaneous and dropped various types of vocals. It was all so personal, all of it. At times I didn't know where my vocals began or ended, or if it was Feist, Kevin, or myself I was hearing. It didn't matter, though. It was moving me.

MURRAY LIGHTBURN_ We had all gone to Japan to do this "Canada Wet" tour: it was Death From Above 1979, Metric, The Dears, BSS, Stars — a pretty spicy little bill. Kevin came up to me and said, "I want you to sing on this song," and it was one of my favourite songs of theirs, "All the Gods." A few months later, we were playing in Toronto and that was when I was supposed to go into Newfeld's studio. I was a bit apprehensive about the whole thing because I'm not a big collaboration guy, and I don't really hang out with Broken Social Scene on a regular basis, mostly because of geography. I couldn't get hold of Newfeld at first, and by the time I actually got to the studio, I was already half in the bag. Of course, Kevin was not there — Broken

Social Scene were on tour in Europe. So the whole scenario made no sense. I sang my harmony part, but what was really weird was that Newfeld also asked me to do all this other really wacky shit — kind of go nuts on a couple of tracks and wail. I could barely make out anything in my headphones — what he played me was pure chaos. I could kind of hear multiple tracks of Feist singing, and she was wailing, and I'm thinking, "This is totally not going to wind up on the record, so I might as well fuck it up."

Next thing I know, [their manager] has the new Social Scene record on her iPod, and that's how I found out the song Kevin originally asked me to do wasn't on the record — it wound up being a seven-inch B-side. Meanwhile, Google News is reporting that I'm all over the record, to the point that I'm part of Broken Social Scene: "Members of Broken Social Scene include Murray Lightburn of The Dears." That's probably what they wanted — to snare another character into their web. It was a really bizarre experience: I'm looking at the track list and I don't recognize anything, and yet I'm somehow still on the record? I remember writing an email to Jeffrey Remedios saying, "I feel totally misrepresented here. I'm clearly not on the record and yet I'm all over the press release."

> *SOMETIMES WHEN MUSICIANS GET TOGETHER TO MAKE MUSIC IT'S LIKE SEX: THERE IS SO MUCH POTENTIAL IN THE IDEA, BUT AT SOME POINT POTENTIAL HAS TO TRANSMUTE INTO PHYSICAL MANIFESTATION.*

AMY MILLAN_ I came in occasionally and did some breathing. I wrote a couple of songs, including "Aging Places/Losing Faces," which is on Kevin's record but was originally supposed to be on the Broken Social Scene record, and [the fast version of] "Major Label Debut," which became the elusive lost song. But it was a time when Stars were also recording and were really busy. So I'd come into town and Emily and I would do some ahhs and eees and errrs and scream — whatever Dave wanted. It was a difficult time; it felt like everything could fall apart, but we managed to get the record out.

*JAMES SHAW_* For me, that record was way less cohesive. It seemed like Kevin was entering a state of personal unrest, and he was much more distracted than he was during the making of the other records. His energy was way more dispersed. I remember feeling like every time I went into the studio, I was kind of itching to get back out again. I wasn't really enjoying the making of that album. It just seemed like if I went in and did something that had everybody raising their hands and saying, "This is fucking incredible," it never showed up on the track. The record is amazing unto itself, but I dare to question how many genius moments were left out.

THERE WAS A DIFFERENT VIBE: IT WAS DARK, ANGRY, MUFFLED, REPRESSED, BETRAYED.

*JO-ANN GOLDSMITH_* There was a different vibe: it was dark, angry, muffled, repressed, betrayed. When things get so out of control and people start telling you you're so much greater than you are, inevitably you start to feel like maybe you're hiding a deep, dark secret that you're not as great as everybody thinks you are. You think to yourself, "All this great success has started happening to you — why aren't you happy? You did everything they told you to do: you became famous, you started making money, you're travelling the world, your life is so exciting — yet you're still unhappy." Relationships were falling apart on a lot of levels for a lot of people, even personal relationships within the band too. I remember Kevin and Justin got into a huge fight in my hallway. The love felt like it was gone. "Blame the president for destroying our marriage" — that was my line, because I joked to Kevin, "We're getting a divorce because George Bush got re-elected." That album was about love lost. Even

though most people listening to the album don't know what it's really about, it's pretty hard that it's out there, the energy and essence of those emotions being transmitted for a million people to hear.

*NADIN BRENDEL_* I believe that great artists have always created their most amazing work in turbulent times. Broken Social Scene, and Kevin in particular, put their hearts onto paper that year, writing some of the most therapeutic lines ever. You see kids rocking out to songs like "Superconnected" — but if they only knew what heartache inspired these lyrics.

*EVAN CRANLEY_* There was definitely a lot more angst involved during this recording, and it was definitely a more personal journey for Brendan and Kevin as bandleaders. And the record's a mess — I like the record, but there are tracks that are almost impossible to listen to. It's true, I'm sorry. There's that track "Our Faces Split the Coast in Half" — that's the sound of anxiety, that's the sound of pressure, that's the sound of things falling apart. There were so many things that were happening in our personal lives that got spit out on that record.

*JAMES SHAW_* I got the sense that Newfeld was trying to pick up the slack for the fact that everyone was so fucked up, and he's not really that kind of guy. He does his best work when there's a lot of structure around him, so when the structure leaves the room for ten minutes, he gets to go crazy. But when he feels the responsibility to manage all this insane shit . . . I don't know if that's his strongest asset.

*JUSTIN PEROFF_* Newf tried to outdo himself, which is reflected in the production on a lot of those songs. Kevin would say, "Turn down my vocals," because he's singing in a whole other fashion and he doesn't know if that's a good thing or a bad thing. So

Where is cyberperume? RIGHT HERE!

thedz ♥ love you guys! a lot!

Give a 110%

Thx for this. ♥

feisty says

...but only if you FEEL like it. → you owe me 110.00$ Fucker

you're just like crosstown traffic... — so hard to get ... to you.

Broken?

Broken Social Scene's tour bus board, 2006. (AW)

THERE WERE SO MANY THINGS THAT WERE HAPPENING IN OUR PERSONAL LIVES THAT GOT SPIT OUT ON THAT RECORD.

Broken Social Scene onstage in Reading, England, 2006. (JS)

you have a producer who wants to outdo himself and a vocalist who doesn't want anybody to hear what he's singing.

*DAVE NEWFELD_* Things first got weird for me when we were signed to Mercury in the U.K. Steve Lillywhite was the A&R overseer, and he had produced "Beautiful Day" by U2. So I went and bought the U2 album so I could hear the mix in my speakers and gauge how far off I was. The funny thing was, the whole reason in the first place everyone got excited about Broken Social Scene was because we had done our stuff without thinking about what was going on in modern music. So I remember that was a whole new way of mixing a tune, where I'm thinking of the track going A/B against a U2 song on the radio.

IF YOU WANT US TO GET PERSONAL, THEN PLAY THE RECORD.

*JEFFREY REMEDIOS_* Kevin has a habit of taking his poppiest hits and producing them in a way that doesn't make them universally appealing, but clearly more interesting. "Superconnected" could've been the next U2 smash; he just took it in a different direction, and at the end of the day, it was a more interesting song.

*TORQUIL CAMPBELL_* I think that album's fucking incredible. I think Newfeld and Kevin were both working so hard and sort of working in opposite directions, and that's what's so beautiful about those two: that tangle of two people who fundamentally understand each other and yet fundamentally don't know what the fuck the other is talking about. It's a unique relationship, and you hear the complicated beauty of all that shit going on in their heads.

*KEVIN DREW[2]_* No one ever wanted to make the big, clean album. It's a record where you come and be a part of it. We're not hiding. That was something that was great about *You Forgot It In People*:

having very heavy moments, but taking people out of them. Like at the end of "Bandwitch," you can hear us talking, it's like, "Come in from the cold — sit down, have some tea, warm up, let me show you this fuckin' ridiculous movie, we're going to hang out and be OK for a while." And that's really important: to contradict all the pain. Because if you just start singing about all the pain, you're no better than the rest of them. The "you and me" songs will take over, and I don't think anyone in this band wanted to have a traditionally lyrical album of "I love you, I miss you, I hate you, I need you." Some heavy shit's addressed, but it's addressed in a manner where we're not going to talk about it, because we can't — it's not ours. If you want us to get personal, then play the record. But I'm not going to tell you a story about my life. Because as my uncle says, "It always involves others," and you've always got to expose others, and that's not right.

*GEORGE VALE_* There were a lot of relationship issues that were going on — some good, some bad. Brendan met [his girlfriend] Sarah [Haywood], and is probably going to be with her for the rest of his life. But a lot of relationships were ending, not just in Broken Social Scene but in other, related bands. It was a hectic summer. It was like somebody either needed to get beat up or killed or married. I regret what happened to Dave in New York . . . It was so hard — I was just standing there talking to the cop with my hands in my pockets, and all of a sudden Dave's getting thumped. I shouldn't have brought Davey there — it was like taking a lamb to slaughter. Dave kind of lost it there for a little while; he got crazy about [the lawsuit]. But he was right — he stuck it out. And he got paid for it, and he paid for his new studio with it, so I don't feel so, so bad about it anymore.

*KEVIN DREW[3]_* It was a horrible, horrible situation to watch a friend go through, and it was a

Clockwise from the left: Kevin Drew, Charles Spearin, Justin Peroff, Evan Cranley, Dave Newfeld, Ohad Benchetrit, Brendan Canning, Amy Millan, Jason Collett, and Andrew Whiteman in a 2005 press shot.

Left to right: Jeffrey Remedios, Brendan Canning, Christian the sound guy, Kevin Drew, Jason Collett, and Andrew Whiteman on tour. (LF)

THERE WERE A LOT OF RELATION-SHIP ISSUES THAT WERE GOING ON —SOME GOOD, SOME BAD.

Broken Social Scene performing in Australia, 2006. (JP)

Drawings from a self-titled booklet by Christopher Mills, coloured in by Brendan Canning. (JPF)

HUNTER

Brendan Canning, 2005. (JPF)

horrible ending to a very fucking hard process [making the record] . . . Social Scene and Newf are done for a while. It kills him. He needs to get some projects where it's just him and a four-piece band — we really took a few years off his life with this one. Because he just puts it all on his sleeve, he tries to get everybody involved and he wants everyone to be heard and he always feels like everybody's breathing down his neck. He makes it all up in his head, of course. You'll be like, "This sounds good, mix it," and then you leave, come back, listen to his mix and you're like, "What the hell is this?"

DAVE NEWFELD_ [Brendan and Kevin] were more bothered with the album than I was. That thing in New York also really pissed them off, even though it wasn't my fault. It was after the self-titled album was done, so that was a period of discontent — everything they thought was not good about their band at the time, they blamed it on me. Basically I was the fall guy. You really saw it in the U.S. press, where they said, "We put up with Dave, and it was really hard." So they were begrudging me in the press, and the reality was, "Dudes, we really worked hard and that album is actually really good. Just because a few people didn't like it — you guys didn't like it at first . . ."

Later, Kevin wrote me a long letter of apology, saying, "I just listened to the album, and it's fucking great. I can't believe I dissed you publicly and undermined the art I was putting out. I was insecure, and I won't do this to you in the European press. It's totally unfair." I still stand by that album — even if it's not everyone's cup of tea, it's a great fucking album. And even though they dissed me in the press, we were always friends. They just don't hold back their discontent. They said they didn't like the album and that set the tone, and the reviewers who picked it apart could say, "We're concurring with the band." How are the fans going to like it if the band doesn't like it?

JAMES SHAW_ I was a little frustrated by the timing of the release, because *Broken Social Scene* was supposed to come out four, five months before, and I said, "Okay, this is all going to work out great." Then all of a sudden, the date kept getting pushed, and then all of a sudden it got pushed right onto our release date [for Metric's *Live It Out*]. And then — cut to three weeks later — I open up *SPIN* magazine and both records get one review together, which was irritating. That's the last time we'll do that!

LESLIE FEIST_ I wasn't around for the making of that album. By that point, it really was clear that Kevin was the de facto leader, but everybody except him and Canning was in other bands. Even Peroff DJs on the side. Then there's Apostle, Jason Collett, Stars, Metric, and Do Makes. So Kevin and Brendan were left with Newfeld in this bunker in downtown Toronto trying to make decisions for the greater good. Everyone else would come in and hear the album with some clarity, having not been there for the whole arduous process — like, why isn't the fast "Major Label Debut" on there? And the reason is because Kevin doesn't want to be a cliché or have a band with just one song that everybody knows, like [Pulp's] "Common People" or [King Missile's] "Detachable Penis."

SO THEY WERE BEGRUDGING ME IN THE PRESS, AND THE REALITY WAS, "DUDES, WE REALLY WORKED HARD AND THAT ALBUM IS ACTUALLY REALLY GOOD. JUST BECAUSE A FEW PEOPLE DIDN'T LIKE IT — YOU GUYS DIDN'T LIKE IT AT FIRST . . ."

BRENDAN CANNING_ Getting Lisa Lobsinger was such a gamble. I liked her voice; she sang really well on her demos — she was right in the perfect range. There was no audition. It was like, "You're flying out here and you're in the band." We made it work.

LISA LOBSINGER_ I wasn't sure if I was auditioning or coming to rehearse. But the whole time I thought I'd be doing four or five Canadian dates, max. And then when I got here, they were like, "No, we're going to the States and Europe!" At the time I had three jobs in Calgary. I actually called all three jobs and said, "Uh, I'm not coming back Monday . . ." That was probably the best feeling in the whole world.

AT TIMES HE'S UNBELIEVABLY COMPASSIONATE, AND AT OTHER TIMES HE'S MADDENINGLY SELF-ABSORBED, TO THE POINT WHERE I JUST WANT TO PUNCH HIM.

JULIE PENNER_ Touring was insane. Some nights I'd think it was one of the best shows I've ever seen and some nights it was a bit of a disaster. Kevin would always try to salvage it because he just knew some of the kids weren't being fooled by the spectacle on those nights. One night in New York, the show wasn't going well, and he just stepped into the crowd and started hugging people. It was Kevin's way of making the most direct connection with the fans as possible.

JOHN CROSSINGHAM_ Kevin's possessed by this incredible self-belief and this crippling self-doubt. At times he's unbelievably compassionate, and at other times he's maddeningly self-absorbed, to the point where I just want to punch him. But he's done some of the most generous things for me, and he does have a really good heart. He is without a doubt the most charismatic person I have ever come into contact with. People love him, and he is very worthy of love. I mean, he's got people like J Mascis calling him up. That's fucked up!

J MASCIS[4]_ I don't remember the first time I heard [Broken Social Scene]; I might've seen the video for "Almost Crimes" first. Other people have said that they sound like Dinosaur Jr. I don't know, it doesn't really occur to me immediately.

GORDON MOAKES_ The first time Broken Social Scene and Bloc Party played together properly was at Olympic Island, and I've never felt so welcomed into another town by a band. It was almost the first time we felt like we could be part of a community of bands in a way, because, growing up and playing in London, there was never any community to it — just competition and bitchiness and endless reams of rubbish bands trying to make it. Later that year we were in L.A. Kevin and Brendan were there and we all had a day off, so Kevin invited us to a friend's house to just have a quiet drink and enjoy a barbecue. It was the least rock 'n' roll moment of all time, just a few guys in a couple of bands taking some time away from the chaos to listen and chat to each other. I was quite moved by how conscientious they were and how friendly.

SCOTT KANNBERG_ I think bands go through the same thing [that he went through in Pavement ten years ago]. A few years ago, Kevin was complaining to me about having to do a college tour through the U.S., and I just said to him, "You don't need to do that; you just did a U.S. tour. You don't need to come back and play secondary markets, especially if you're burned out already. The bookings will still be there." The next thing I knew, he cancelled the tour! I felt bad. But for me, Pavement did every single thing, and we got really burned out. So I see bands doing a lot of the same things, but hopefully they learn.

BRENDAN CANNING_ There wasn't really a refresher time between [*You Forgot It In People* and *Broken Social Scene*], so we went on fumes for a long time. That last U.S. tour [in the fall of 2006], we fought almost daily over whether to do it; meanwhile, we should've been fighting over the tour before that or all those shit European tours. You do great in London and Dublin and Glasgow and Berlin and Barcelona and Madrid, but anywhere

Justin Peroff on the tour bus, 2005. (AW)

THERE WAS NEVER AN END DATE MARKED ON OUR CALENDAR . . .

Andrew Whiteman onstage at Lollapalooza in Chicago, 2006. (JS)

Top, left to right: Lil' Jaz, Justin Peroff, and k-os, 2006. (DR)

Charles Spearin and Brendan Canning in London, England, 2006. (JP)

Lisa Lobsinger, 2006. (SH)

else . . . you don't want to spend too much time in provincial areas unless you're a really big band. To keep going and continually touring there, the gratification just is not there.

*JUSTIN PEROFF_* There was never an end date marked on our calendar . . . We were supposed to go on hiatus well before our last show in Ann Arbor [in November 2006], but Brendan was like, "No, we need to do one last tour." Honestly, it was partly financial, and I think it just made sense: when you tour a record, you do North America as a market. What happened was we spent too much time in Europe. Doing that last U.S. tour was a little gruelling, but to see the size of the venues . . . It was great to play two sold-out shows at the Henry Fonda Theater [in L.A.] and walk away on your hiatus really satisfied. I met Lindsay Lohan, which was pretty funny, and played a sold-out tour and completed the cycle by bringing J Mascis and Spiral Stairs onstage. I walked away totally satisfied, and could enjoy the hiatus comfortably.

*ANDREW WHITEMAN_* After that Ann Arbor show . . . That's tough for me to talk about. But what a great tour to be on for the last tour — I found great refuge amongst Do Make Say Think. Note the ever-present wine bottle glued to my right hand. Basically, from the time we toured the States with Feist [in fall 2005] to a year later with the Do Makes, I was a caricature — like "me and my shadow" — in that it was predictable that I would have a bottle of wine. But I wasn't playing a role; I was just getting through life.

A SUPER-CONNECTED TIME TO LEAVE

PUTTING THE "US" IN HIATUS

THE TORONTO THAT SPAWNED Broken Social Scene in 2000 doesn't exist any-more. The Mockingbird and Ted's Wrecking Yard are both long gone. Royal City broke up in 2004; their label, Three Gut Records, folded in 2006, after Tyler Burke left to further her visual-arts career and Lisa Moran decamped to New York to work for Sufjan Stevens's management team. Constantines' Bry Webb and Steve Lambke moved to Montreal. The Hidden Cameras' Joel Gibb moved to Berlin. Dave Newfeld closed Stars and Sons and, with the settlement he received from the NYPD, began to build a new studio in a converted chapel ninety minutes east of Toronto in Trenton, Ontario.

Wavelength is still a going concern, having relocated from Ted's to the reborn Sneaky Dee's in 2002. Perhaps in reaction to indie-rock's increased mainstream popularity and the proliferation of similarly styled showcase nights, its program-ming has become even more adventurous, unpredictable, and culturally diverse. However, attendance has been more inconsistent in recent years while swankier, more fashionista-friendly bars and venues, like the Drake Hotel, Wrongbar, The Beaconsfield, and the Social, in the increasingly active West Queen West corridor, attract the city's trend-spotting hipster hordes.

But then the Broken Social Scene that Toronto spawned is not really here either. The success of a local music scene — the ability of bands to build their audi-ence, sell out shows, and attract international recognition — is ultimately (and par-adoxically) measured by the amount of time its leading ambassadors spend away from it. And yet, even in their absence from the local club circuit, Broken Social

Scene have achieved a different kind of ubiquity. Instead of seeing them play for one hundred people every month at Ted's Wrecking Yard, we hear them in the background at supermarkets and cafés, in TV ads and over movie credits, and during climactic sex scenes on *Nip/Tuck* and *Queer as Folk*.

In that sense, Broken Social Scene were everywhere in 2007 — just not together. Feist released her third album, *The Reminder*, which, on the strength of the single "1234," catapulted her from the next big thing to *the* thing, landing her everywhere from iPod commercials to *Saturday Night Live* to a date at the 2008 Grammy Awards, for which she earned four nominations. Stars boldly stepped out of the BSS mothership's shadow once and for all with their fourth album, *In Our Bedroom After the War*, which generated a heap of pre-release publicity when Arts & Crafts made downloads of the album available for sale online, three months before its retail street date in September. That November, the band sold out four nights in a row at the Phoenix Concert Theatre in Toronto, suggesting that the gambit had paid off.

The year also saw acclaimed new albums from Apostle of Hustle (*National Anthem of Nowhere*), Do Make Say Think (*You, You're a History in Rust*), Raising the Fawn (*Sleight of Hand*), and Emily Haines's solo project, the Soft Skeleton (*What Is Free to a Good Home?*, whose release coincided with that of an anthology of her late father Paul's poetry, *Secret Carnival Workers*). And to that list of extracurricular projects we can add Kevin Drew's debut solo album, *Spirit If . . .* , which was recorded at Ohad Benchetrit's home studio between 2005 and 2007 and released under the banner "Broken Social Scene Presents: Kevin Drew." Guests on the album include Drew's heroes Scott Kannberg, J Mascis, and — proving membership in Broken Social Scene knows no bounds — Canadian rock-radio fixture Tom Cochrane. Brendan Canning released a similarly branded solo album, *Something For All of Us*, in the summer of 2008, featuring contributions from Drew, Justin Peroff, Lisa Lobsinger, and James Shaw, but recorded mostly in collaboration with non-BSS friends Ryan Kondrat and John Lamagna.

In the fall of 2007, Drew toured *Spirit If . . .* under the Broken Social Scene banner, but the band was radically altered from what fans had grown accustomed to. While Drew, Canning, and Peroff still represented the nucleus, the lineup was rounded out by new recruits Andrew Kenny (of Brooklyn-via-Austin indie-rock faves American Analog Set), Sam Goldberg (formerly of Toronto post-punk band Uncut), and Mitch Bowden (a last-minute replacement for Bill Priddle, who injured himself during the tour's opening dates). Definitive BSS characteristics — rotating female singers, a horn section, orchestral crescendos — were forsaken for a more stream-lined presentation that better suited the stripped-down, emotionally direct nature of Drew's album.

But the revamped lineup stays true to the band's original ethos: Broken Social Scene was, and still is, Kevin Drew, Brendan Canning, and whoever's willing to help out. And on the night of December 11, 2007, at a Jason Collett gig at Toronto's Dakota Tavern, that supporting cast once again included James Shaw and Andrew Whiteman, who joined Drew and Canning for an unannounced — and completely improvised — opening set. Seven years, three albums, and countless reviews, inter-views, world tours, makeups, and breakups removed from their Ted's Wrecking Yard genesis, Broken Social Scene are still very much, in the words of Jason Collett, "an experiment in intimacy." And even when solo careers or personal pressures demand a period of separation . . . well, as Drew sings on his solo album's closing track, "You think it's a start, but it's really just the beginning."

IT'S ALL ABOUT THE FRIENDS — THAT'S THE ONLY REASON I WORK WITH THE BAND.

Broken Social Scene photo shoot in London, England, 2003. (JPF)

Leslie Feist and Kevin Drew, 2007. (SH)

*DAVE NEWFELD_* I couldn't have stayed in Stars and Sons renting all my life, and you can't buy a semi-detached house in Toronto south of Bloor for under $400,000. And I don't go out a lot anyway, so I may as well be in the country. I don't go to The Beaconsfield, I don't go to the Social. That doesn't excite me — going into a room where everyone's standing around drinking beer for seven bucks a pop with loud tunes playing in the background. Now I'm only an hour and a half outside Toronto. But I own my place, and I've got windows coming out of my ying yang. I've got this big house that can accommodate seven people. At Stars and Sons, I didn't even have a waiting room and I slept in the boiler room. I didn't have one window in my fucking place for the past eight years. Now I'm in this thirty-foot-ceiling cathedral, and next door is this seven-bedroom house with a massive living room and dining room and three-piece kitchen and laundry and a big cellar on a one-acre lot. I never could've done that in Toronto.

*MARTY KINACK_* I never picked this career; I never dreamt of being in a band or producing records or being on the road. I appreciate everything. It's all about the friends — that's the only reason I work with the band. This year I got offered a bunch of tours to do, like the Bloc Party tour — some pretty successful bands — and I'm like, "I don't know you guys. Want to come to my house for a barbecue, and I'll check you out?" And the managers are like, "We'll send you a full package with CDs and DVDs." And I'm like, "Don't bother — I'm not going to listen or look. Send 'em over for a barbecue. We'll have some margaritas, and I'll let you know."

*JOHN CROSSINGHAM_* I feel like Broken Social Scene is this weird sort of convergence of my greatest successes and my worst decisions. If you look at Social Scene press photos, there were a bunch of photos taken when I was an active member of the band, and I'm not in them. I always feel, from the outsider's point of view, that I am less involved with the band than I really have been. And I do take great comfort in the fact that Kevin and Brendan would both back that up. I do feel like it's something I've always had to fight for because I don't travel in the same social circles. But some of the most incredible, most fulfilling moments I've ever had have been on a stage with those people.

*LESLIE FEIST_* Broken Social Scene will be a band even when we're old and grey, even if it's just at a potluck, because it was never something that needed to be defined.

*SCOTT KANNBERG_* One of the things I really like about the band is the sense of mystery. It's a lot harder to maintain that aura these days, with the Internet. In the old days it took a lot to figure out what the story was. I still think Broken Social Scene have a little bit of that mystery. I think people are still slightly confused about what Broken Social Scene really is. Especially this [solo] thing, "Broken Social Scene Presents: Kevin Drew" — it's like, what the fuck? But I understand why he did it. People who are record-buying fans are easily confused.

> *I FEEL LIKE BROKEN SOCIAL SCENE IS THIS WEIRD SORT OF CONVERGENCE OF MY GREATEST SUCCESSES AND MY WORST DECISIONS. IF YOU LOOK AT SOCIAL SCENE PRESS PHOTOS, THERE WERE A BUNCH OF PHOTOS TAKEN WHEN I WAS AN ACTIVE MEMBER OF THE BAND, AND I'M NOT IN THEM.*

*KEVIN DREW_* Kids don't care about felt-covered albums; all they care about is the music, because that's all they have time for. They don't give a shit about packaging. If they want to read the lyrics they can go online. In the society that we live in now, music is presented with the idea of "Is the song good?" And that's what counts. It's an MP3 world.

[*You Forgot It In People*] was the introduction to that mixed-tape idea. When it first came out, I didn't understand [the concept of] shuffle, the iPod — they did not exist. Cut to 2008, just six years later, and there's been a whole radical change: the way you listen to music, the way music is sold, the way products are consumed, the idea of how much information is involved, the idea of how communication is even more extreme. Kids grow up with machine-gun video games and the ballads [on their cell-phones]. You can't present something that says, "Go home, light a candle, do some meditation, pull out the record, read about the record, put it on, and then see what happens."

I REALLY HAVE NO IDEA WHAT'S GOING TO HAPPEN WITH THE BAND. I HAVE A GREAT RELATIONSHIP WITH KEVIN, WHITEY, AND BRENDAN. I WOULD LOVE TO MAKE MUSIC WITH THEM, AND I KNOW THEY WOULD LOVE TO MAKE MUSIC WITH ME . . . I'M SURE IT'S GOING TO HAPPEN; I JUST DON'T KNOW IN WHAT CAPACITY.

JEFFREY REMEDIOS_ We have to get music to people the way people want their music. All the traditional ways to discover music have been redefined. The need for a major-label distributor is becoming less and less essential because we can do all the distribution ourselves [online]. The green-haired mohawked retail clerk is no longer a barrier to a yuppie discovering music. This entire business that we're in is getting won and lost by fans discovering music one-to-one. Arts & Crafts put the new Stars record out digitally; the next day we announced the tour, which you can buy tickets to only on our website. At the same time we're announcing new merchandise and designs, which you can also buy only from our website. We work pretty tirelessly to always think of the fans first. We're the most transparent arbiters of that relationship between artist and fan.

AMY MILLAN_ I think we [Broken Social Scene] are going to make our best record in a couple of years. All of us will go to a farm or commune. We'll have babies, so we won't want to tour anyway. We'll all just move to Dave Newfeld's house in the country. Evan and I have already started planning our party tent.

OHAD BENCHETRIT_ Broken Social Scene relies on so many people, and they've all gone in different directions and some of them are really successful: Stars, Metric, Feist . . . What makes Social Scene the Social Scene is the idea of this collective being really tight-knit. So the question is whether enough of these people can stop long enough and focus long enough to really get together and continue Social Scene. I don't know, man, I really don't know. I think there's enough core interest, but again, it's not really a core that makes Broken Social Scene Broken Social Scene. Kevin and Brendan can get back in a room together, but is that still truly Social Scene in the larger sense? I think there's still enough love for the band that those who are involved are going to try to make a real strong effort to get those who were involved back into it.

CHARLES SPEARIN_ I really have no idea what's going to happen with the band. I have a great relationship with Kevin, Whitey, and Brendan. I would love to make music with them, and I know they would love to make music with me . . . I'm sure it's going to happen; I just don't know in what capacity. The Broken Social Scene attention should die off pretty soon — I think it's healthy for things to have a good start, blossom, and then go away before they become artificial.

EMILY HAINES_ Every interview I've ever fucking done has asked, "Is Broken Social Scene breaking up?" But you can't break something that's already broken! It's broken, it's permanently broken. The only way you could destroy it would be to actually fix it!

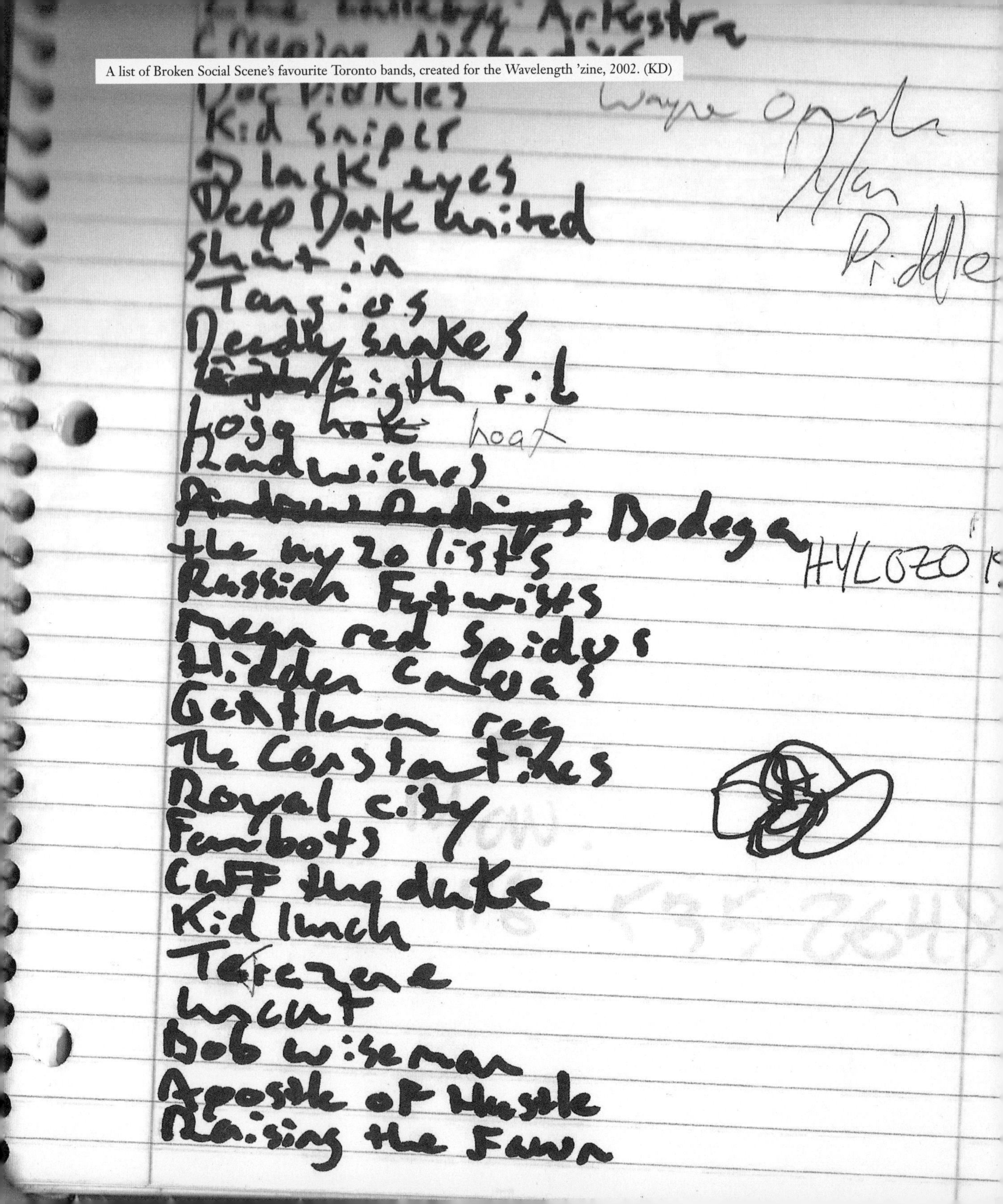

... Lullaby Arkestra

Creeping Nobodies

Doc Pickles

Kid Sniper

Black eyes

Deep Dark United

Shut in

Tangiers

Deadly Snakes

Eighth rib

hoss hot roast

sandwiches

the my 20 lists

Russian Futurists

Mean red spidys

Hidden cameras

Gentleman reg

The Constantines

Royal city

Fembots

Cuff the duke

Kid lunch

Tarezene

wucut

Bob wiseman

Apostle of Hustle

Raising the Fawn

Wayne Omaha

Tyler Priddle

Bodega

HYLOZO'K

TORQUIL CAMPBELL_ The name of the band is so self-fulfilling. All of our bands have been made better and we've been made more important and we've had longer careers and had more luck because of each other. And I don't want to ever lose that, because that's what I have that's unique from other bands: I'm a part of this scene and I know these people. Other than that, I'm just another white dude in an indie-rock band.

ANDREW WHITEMAN_ I've had wrist problems throughout my career, and there was a period when my wrist was really fucking up on me and I couldn't practise. I remember watching Jim Jarmusch's Neil Young movie [*Year of the Horse*], and I almost started crying, because I thought, "What if I don't get to play with these guys?" My dream is to play with these guys in thirty years, playing the fucking "Cause" when we're old men, and it'll sound like fourteen Sonic Youths coming to kill you.

JASON COLLETT_ I've had some of the best times of my life touring with those guys. I know everything's changed; it's not going to be the same. But I think it'll be really great because there's such a diversity of talent in the band. We've barely begun really to explore what the band's capable of. With all the solo stuff happening right now, I think it'll be a really healthy thing for the band to come back together.

EMILY HAINES_ My father was a huge influence on my life. I grew up in a small town in a house that was the world that we lived in. Nobody ever came there, but my dad was constantly connected to people like [U.K. musician/Soft Machine founder] Robert Wyatt. They had only met twice but they had some intense times together and maintained this friendship based on music. This was pre-Internet, so there was this sense of connectivity on a different plane. For whatever reason, my parents —

having lived in New York and been a part of the action there with [jazz musicians like] Albert Ayler — always felt like they were more connected when they removed themselves and then reconnected. I have the same relationship with Toronto as a city as I do with everyone in Broken Social Scene. It's definitely the foundation of my life, but if I'm too close to it, I can't see it. I need a certain distance to actually connect properly with all those people while writing together in the studio and playing shows together. I need that distance in order to maintain my own character and not become interchangeable with Amy and Leslie, because we're all very different. I can go as far out as I want, I can go away forever, but I can't escape this band — which is why I can't be too close to it. It's the one immutable thing I know, and it's what Kevin and I said by the pool when we were seventeen years old: it's a pact, and you can't get out of it.

I HAVE THE SAME RELATIONSHIP WITH TORONTO AS A CITY AS I DO WITH EVERYONE IN BROKEN SOCIAL SCENE. IT'S DEFINITELY THE FOUNDATION OF MY LIFE, BUT IF I'M TOO CLOSE TO IT, I CAN'T SEE IT.

JAMES SHAW_ When I was on the last Metric tour, I sat down in the front lounge and turned on the television and watched the last half of [the Neil Young concert film] *Heart of Gold*. I saw what I perceived to be one man's relationship with dozens and dozens of other musicians, and dozens and dozens of records, and a whole life in the music industry, being able to get up onstage and perform. Not just the songs, but the relationships. He's standing beside Emmylou Harris — those two have known each other a long, long time, and I'm sure they've had ups and downs and all sorts of crap that we all think in our own self-centred worlds is so unique to us, but it really, genuinely isn't. I think that I'd like to see us all on stage in twenty-five years, playing new songs and old songs and revelling in our lives together without letting personal shit get in the way.

BRENDAN CANNING_ I don't know how long bands are supposed to play together. It's not like Miles Davis had the same band for a long time. He continued his journey. So many bands think, "We've got our sound, we're making money, people like it." You sort of rely on that; it's human nature. But familiarity will always breed contempt. Everyone gets sick of everyone eventually. But at least this band shifts a little bit.

KEVIN DREW_ There was always something about everyone in this band. I have an extreme attraction to Andrew, to Jason, to Justin, to Brendan, to Amy, Leslie, Emily, Jimmy, Charles, Ohad, Evan, Johnny . . . I'm drawn to my friends. It's been a curse for me. I was that idiot who fell in love with everybody and just wanted every one of them separately to myself at some point. I knew at a young age that I needed good friends because they were going to become everything to me. I was with Jo-Ann because of that. My problem is that I love these people way too much and it fucked me up. I just believed in everyone who stood beside me whenever the lights went up and the crowd roared. Every member of Broken Social Scene gave me something that I wanted in my own performance, examples of how I wanted to push my own views and passion musically. Though I haven't listened to *You Forgot It In People* in years, I know that the only reason I gave every performance I did was because of who I was making music with. Most musicians strive for that with three people, but I found myself with ten or eleven people. There were times when I thought, "How is this possible?"

The genuine, real approach to how it came together — you can never capture a friendship on film, in a song, or in words. You just can't. And we're fucking friends because we've hated each other at points and we've fucking adored each other at points. That's why no one, nothing, no book, no interview, no description in front of a camera — nothing will ever, ever explain the sense of community that was cultivated by this band. Nothing. It will never come across the way that it's supposed to.

2008 set list. (JPF)

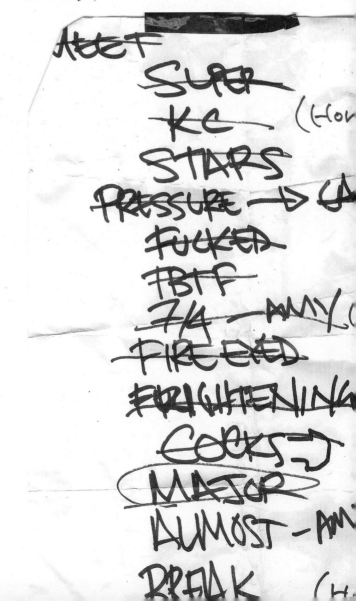

Kevin Drew and Andrew Whiteman with "Let's make love" and "I'm a virgin" projections on their backs in London, England, 2003. (LF)

Broken Social Scene's logo. (JPF)

EPILOGUE

IT WAS A GIVEN that the Broken Social Scene story would continue to evolve in unexpected ways, and that any ending I could give it would be inherently premature. The challenge, then, was to select an end point that didn't feel arbitrary, and the winter of 2007–08 seemed as good a time as any to bring the story of Broken Social Scene to, if not a close, then a reflective pause.

Kevin Drew had just released his solo album; Brendan Canning was finishing his. Andrew Whiteman was in the midst of a year-long leave from the band. Stars went on tour for what seemed like forever. Jason Collett was about to issue his third solo effort, *Here's to Being Here*. James Shaw built a coach-house recording complex called Giant Studios (with his neighbour, Sebastien Grainger, formerly of Death From Above 1979) to give Metric a base of operations for their next album. And Feist, of course, was busy being Feist, accumulating increasingly surreal markers of mainstream fame: *Sesame Street* appearances, *MAD-TV* parodies, *Colbert Report* skits, and an invitation to join a BBC-commissioned envoy to study the effects of global warming in the Arctic.

What wasn't entirely expected was that, from the time of my submitting the manuscript in January 2008 to the book being designed that summer, Broken Social Scene would undergo arguably its most intense period of activity to date. The fall 2007 touring schedule for Kevin Drew's *Spirit If . . .* album effectively bled into the summer 2008 itinerary for Brendan Canning's *Something for All of Us*, with Whiteman reinstituted into the lead-guitarist role, and Liz Powell of Montreal indie-rock trio Land of Talk recruited to provide the band with a new female voice.

Arts & Crafts, meanwhile, went on a signing frenzy — or perhaps you could call it a rescue mission — as the label picked up long-time BSS associates the Constantines, Gonzalez, The Stills, and Gentleman Reg, providing the artists with much-needed promotional muscle in North America.

And yet, by the end of 2008, the future of Broken Social Scene seemed as uncertain as ever. At a suitably shambolic, three-hour concert in Brooklyn's Masonic Temple in October 2008, Drew prefaced the closing performance of "It's All Gonna Break" by claiming it would be the last time we would hear a lot of these old BSS standards, that the band was due for a hiatus, and that if there was going to be a next tour, it would likely take the form of a revue-style showcase spotlighting individual members' solo projects. But just three weeks later, I found myself in Giant Studios with Drew, Canning, Justin Peroff, Ohad Benchetrit, and Charles Spearin, listening to an electronic disco-funk jam the guys had just recorded. Who knows if the track signals a new direction for the band, or if they were just goofing around. And if and when the band gets around to completing another album, who knows who will be involved — if it will feature the twelve-person mob that figured on Broken Social Scene's early albums, or the leaner line-ups seen on the more recent solo-album tours.

As ever, the only thing certain about Broken Social Scene is that everything about them exists in a permanent temporary state. This is my third attempt at writing an epilogue to make this book as up-to-date as possible — and yet right after I send this draft to my editor, I half expect to receive news from Kevin and Brendan of some new side project or celebrity collaboration or sabbatical to Mexico or inter-band romance/break-up that will re-route the band's trajectory once again, and force another re-write.

For now at least, I can safely say this book is over. But the story most certainly isn't.

BROKEN SOCIAL SCENE
SETLIST
11/09/06 // Last Show Ever.

LOVERS

7/4

FIRE-EYED BOY

CAUSE = TIME

STARS AND SONS

SUPER

USA

HANDJOBS

ANTHEMS FOR A ...

HOTEL

LOOKS LIKE THE SUN

COLLETT'S JAM

IBI

MAJOR

ALMOST

BANDWITCH

PACIFIC

BREAK

KC

NOT.

Broken Social Scene's "Last Show Ever" set list, Ann Arbor, Michigan, November 2006. (LB)

at the CAMERON house

in this order · from 10pm

① JULIAN BROWN
③ ILSE GUDIÑO
④ ANDREW WHITEMAN
② WILL FORD afro percussion ensemble
⑤ MIKO SOBRIERA
⑥ OTTO CLOK
⑦ LESLIE FEIST

bux

Do
MAKE
SAY
thinK
315
Queen St.
EAST
Church At
Berkley.
JUNe 15

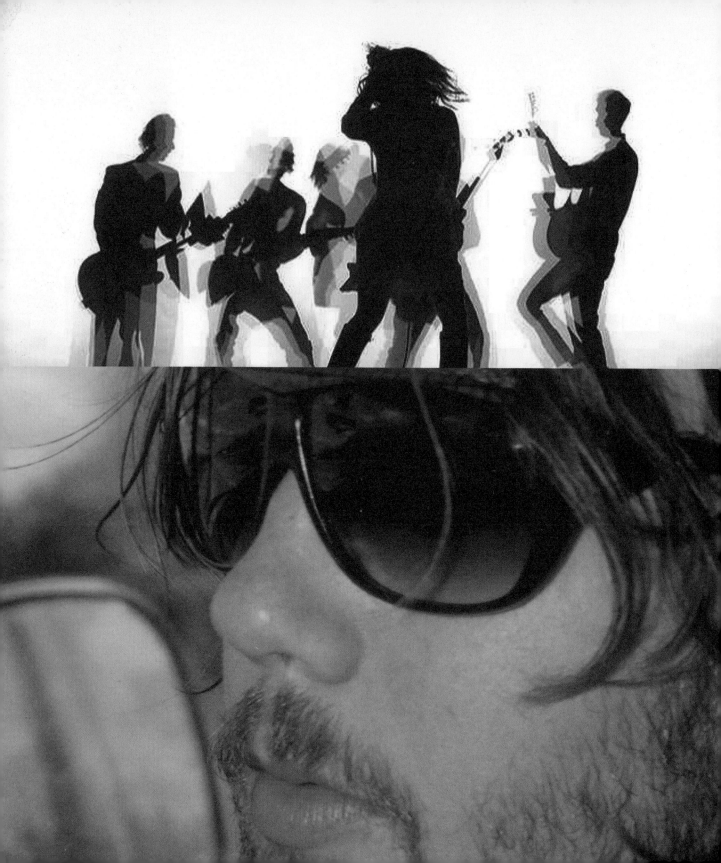

NOTES

CHAPTER 2: WE COLLIDE

[1] Interview for *TORO* magazine, March 2003.
[2] Interview for *TORO* magazine, March 2003.

CHAPTER 5: I BELIEVE IN THE GOOD LIFE

[1] Interview for *TORO* magazine, March 2003.
[2] Ibid.
[3] "Constant Craving," *Eye Weekly*, February 15, 2001.
[4] Interview for *TORO* magazine, March 2003.

CHAPTER 6: LOVE AND MATHEMATICS

[1] Interview for *Eye Weekly*, December 2002.
[2] "Made To Be Broken," *Eye Weekly*, December 12, 2002.

CHAPTER 7: THEY ALL WANT TO BE THE CAUSE

[1] Interview for *Eye Weekly*, December 2002.
[2] Ibid.
[3] Ibid.
[4] Ibid.
[5] "Made To Be Broken," *Eye Weekly*, December 12, 2002.

CHAPTER 8: MAJOR LABEL DEBUT

[1] Interview for *Report on Business* magazine, July 2007.
[2] Ibid.

CHAPTER 9: ALL MY FRIENDS IN MAGAZINES

[1] "Made To Be Broken," *Eye Weekly*, December 12, 2002.

CHAPTER 10: IT'S ALL GONNA BREAK

[1] Interview for *TORO* magazine, June 2005.
[2] Ibid.
[3] Ibid.
[4] Interview with *Eye Weekly*, June 2006.

PHOTOGRAPHY CREDITS

Every reasonable effort has been made to trace ownership of copyright materials. The publisher will gladly rectify any inadvertent errors or omissions in credits in future editions.

ap — all photos
t — top
tc — top centre
tl — top left
tr — top right
trc — top right-hand corner
cl — centre left
cr — centre right
b — bottom
bl — bottom left
br — bottom right

AD — Amit Dahan: 3, t, bl; 4, trc, cr; 7, t; 50, b; 67; 69, b; 71, r; 72, ap; 74, t

AK — Andrew Kenny: viii, t

AM — Courtesy of Amy Millan: 158, tr, b; 159, bl

AW — Courtesy of Andrew Whiteman: 127, ap; 131, t; 137, t; 163, br

BC — Courtesy of Brendan Canning: 21, 29

CB — Cecilia Berkovic: x, br

CC — Carlos Carbonell/Houston Party Records: 155

CG — Chris Grismer: 159, br

CM — Christopher Mills: 156, t

CR — Constellation Records: 52, tr

CS — Courtesy of Charles Spearin: 49; 50, t

DR — Dustin Rabin: 138, t

EH — Courtesy of Emily Haines: 39; 40, ap; 159, tr

GV — George Vale: xiii, t; 119, t; 154, t; 164, t

JM — Courtesy of Jane Millan: 20; 35; 37, ap; 52, tl

JP — Julie Penner: vii, t; 128, t; 133, b; 138, b; 154, b

JPF — Artwork by Justin Peroff; photos, press clippings, and set lists courtesy of Justin Peroff: viii, br; x, tr; xii; xv, ap; 3, br; 10; 62; 69, t; 81; 85, br; 86; 93; 95; 98, ap; 101; 102; 105; 108, ap; 111, bl, br; 113, ap; 115, ap; 120; 121; 123; 128, bl; 134, ap; 144, t; 149; 150, b; 156, b; 159, tl; 164, b

JR — Courtesy of Jeffrey Remedios: xvi–xvii; 116; 119, b; 156, b; 165

JS — Courtesy of James Shaw: vii, b; 112; 131, b; 137, b

JSM — Courtesy of Justin Small: 162, tr

KD — Courtesy of Kevin Drew: xi, t; 43; 45, ap; 47, b; 71, tl; 147

LB — Lauren Baker: 153

LF — Courtesy of Leslie Feist: vi, b; 47, t; 111, t; 133, tr; 150, t; 158, tl

MD — Maggie Drew: 157, b

NFR — Noise Factory Records: 52, b

NW — Norman Wong: 163, l

OZ — Olga Zmiejko: x, bl

PW — Paula Wilson: 83

RV — Rachel Verbin: x, tl; 128, br

SB — Courtesy of Stuart Berman/*Eye Weekly*: 13; 15, b; 27, b; 85, cr

SC — Stephen Chung: xi, b; xiii, b; 18; 25, ap; 27, t; 71, bl; 74, b; 78–79; 85, t, bl; 91, ap; 162, b

SF — Courtesy of the Spearin family: viii, bl; 157, tl, tr; 162, tl; 163, tr, cr

SH — Sarah Haywood: vi, t; ix; xiv; 9, t; 139; 141; 144, b

SK — Sandy Kim: 17

TCB — Courtesy of Tyler Clark Burke: 23; 30; 55; 57, ap; 58, ap; 61, ap; 65, ap

TW — Todd Wilson: 15, t

ACKNOWLEDGEMENTS

Stuart Berman thanks Broken Social Scene and all the interview subjects for their time, participation, and stories; Cam Drew for making it all happen; Justin Peroff for the visual inspiration; David Drew for the swift administration; Lauren Baker for the patience (I owe you several weekend afternoon strolls); *Eye Weekly* for the time off; Simon White for the Bloc Party hookup; Sarah MacLachlan, Lynn Henry, and Janie Yoon at Anansi for helping make sense of it all; and Bill Douglas for a beautiful design that truly reflects Broken Social Scene's chaotic but loving nature. For anyone seeking a more extensive history of Canadian independent music, I highly recommend *Have Not Been the Same: The CanRock Renaissance* by Michael Barclay, Ian A. D. Jack, and Jason Schneider — a valuable text that informed the first chapter of this book.

Apologies to those whom I initially approached for interviews but, for whatever reason, failed to connect with. This band is hardly lacking for friends and associates with interesting stories to tell, but when you factor in a day job, word counts, and deadlines (and the desire to maintain some semblance of a social life), there are only so many evenings and weekends to transcribe them.

Thanks especially to Kevin Drew, Brendan Canning, and Jeffrey Remedios for granting me a front-row seat to the soundtrack of my life for the past seven years.

ABOUT THE AUTHOR

STUART BERMAN is an editor at *Eye Weekly*, and has been writing about the Toronto music scene for ten years. His writing on music and pop culture has appeared in PitchforkMedia.com, *Magnet*, *The Village Voice*, *Toro*, *Azure*, the *Toronto Star*, and the *National Post*. He is also the lead singer of The Two Koreas, a garage rock band that, at last count, included no members of Broken Social Scene. He lives in Toronto.

ADDITIONAL CAPTIONS

Page vi, top; left to right: Brendan Canning, Leslie Feist, and Kevin Drew outside the Ed Sullivan Theater in New York City, August 2007. (SH)

Page vi, bottom; left to right: Kevin Drew, Charles Spearin, and Andrew Whiteman in Montreal, 2003. (LF)

Page vii, top: Kevin Drew at London, England's, Koko Theatre, May 2006. (JP)

Page vii, bottom: Stage set-up at Virgin Festival on Toronto Island, 2006. (JS)

Page viii, top: Justin Peroff on drums, 2007. (AK)

Page viii, bottom left: Evan Cranley, Charles Spearin, Jo-Ann Goldsmith, Torquil Campbell, and Chris Seligman at the Phoenix Concert Theatre, 2003. (SF)

Page viii, bottom right: Jason Collett and Brendan Canning, Anytown USA, 2003. (JPF)

Page ix: Brendan Canning in New York City, 2007 (SH)

Page x, top left: Leslie Feist at Kool Haus, 2006. (RV)

Page x, top right: Andrew Whiteman, 2006. (JPF)

Page x, bottom left: Justin Peroff, 2007. (OZ)

Page x, bottom right: Graffiti on the bathroom wall at the Phoenix Concert Theatre, 2003. (CB)

Page xi, top: Kevin Drew's credit notes for *You Forgot It In People*, 2002. (KD)

Page xi, bottom: Brendan Canning, Emily Haines, and Kevin Drew, 2005. (SC)

Page xii: Poster for a Broken Social Scene show at the Horseshoe Tavern, 2002. (JPF)

Page xiii, top: Brendan Canning at home in Toronto, 2005. (GV)

Page xiii, bottom: Brendan Canning and Kevin Drew performing at Soundscapes, 2002. (SC)

Page xiv: 2006 set list (SH)

Page xv, top: Kevin Drew in New York City, 2003. (JPF)

Page xv, bottom: Brendan Canning in New York City, 2003. (JPF)

Page xvi–xvii: Broken Social Scene with Stars, Metric, The Dears, and Death From Above 1979 at the Liquid Room in Tokyo, Japan, 2005 (JR)

Page 13: Ads for the Horseshoe Tavern and the Rivoli, featuring The Rheostatics and hHead, 1998. (SB)

Page 23: Leslie Feist, 1999. (TCB)

Page 35, left to right: Amy Millan and Emily Haines performing at the Horseshoe Tavern with Edith's Mission, 1996. (JM)

Page 43: Kevin Drew on tour with Do Make Say Think, 2000. (KD)

Page 55: The crowd at the Three Gut Records launch, 1999. (TCB)

Page 67: Broken Social Scene performing at Ted's Wrecking Yard, 2001. (AD)

Pages 81 and 95: The second-edition cover art for *You Forgot It In People*. (JPF)

Page 102: *You Forgot It In People* album credits. (JPF)

Page 105: Broken Social Scene on the cover of the *Austin Chronicle*, 2004. (JPF)

Page 115, clockwise from top left-hand corner: Broken Social Scene featured in *Dazed and Confused*, August 2003; *Time Out*, June 2003; *GQ*, November 2003; *Rolling Stone*, June 2003; Pitchfork's rave review of *You Forgot It In People*, 2002; *New York Times Magazine*, 2006. (JPF)

Page 123: Andrew Whiteman and Kevin Drew, 2005. (JPF)

Page 141: Andrew Whiteman's fingers post-show, 2007. (SH)

Page 154, top; left to right: Charles Spearin, Brendan Canning, Kevin Drew, Rush's Geddy Lee, Justin Peroff, and Ohad Benchetrit at the "Fire Eye'd Boy" video shoot in Toronto, 2005. (GV)

Page 154, bottom: Justin Peroff and John Crossingham in Europe, 2005. (JP)

Page 155: Kevin Drew onstage in 2005. (CC)

Page 156, top: Drawing from a self-titled booklet by Christopher Mills, coloured in by Kevin Drew, 2004. (CM)

Page 156, bottom: Brendan Canning in Austin, Texas, 2003. (JR)

Page 157, top left: Charles Spearin playing guitar, 2004. (SF)

Page 157, top right; left to right: Charles Spearin, Susie Spearin, and Ohad Benchetrit, with families, 2004. (SF)

Page 157, bottom, left to right: Amy Millan, Leslie Feist, David Drew, and Emily Haines. (MD)

Page 158, top left: Jason Collett and Leslie Feist in Toronto, February 2003. (LF)

Page 158, top right: Evan Cranley on the road, 2004. (AM)

Page 158, bottom: Broken Social Scene and Stars in Europe, 2004. (AM)

Page 159, top left: Apostle of Hustle variety-show poster, Toronto, 2002. (JPF)

Page 159, top right: Emily Haines and James Shaw of Metric, 2000. (EH)

Page 159, bottom left: Emily Haines with Amy Millan and Torquil Campbell of Stars, 2003. (AM)

Page 159, bottom right: Emily Haines and Kevin Drew, 2004. (CG)

Pages 160–61: Torquil Campbell and Amy Millan, 2004.

Page 162, top left: Charles Spearin, Jason Collett, Andrew Whiteman, and Leslie Feist, 2003. (SF)

Page 162, top right: Do Make Say Think poster, Toronto, 2001. (JSM)

Page 162, bottom: Kevin Drew and Brendan Canning, 2003. (SC)

Page 163, left: J Mascis and Kevin Drew onstage, 2006 (NW)

Page 163, top right: Jason Collett strumming on his guitar, 2004. (SF)

Page 163, centre right: Brendan Canning, 2004. (SF)

Page 163, bottom right: Justin Peroff and Andrew Whiteman, 2006. (AW)

Page 164, top: A scene from Broken Social Scene's "Almost Crimes" music video, 2003. (GV)

Page 164, bottom: Kevin Drew, 2003. (JPF)

Page 165: Leslie Feist, Justin Peroff, and Brendan Canning, 2003. (JR)

Clockwise from top left-hand corner: Jason Collett and Kevin Drew; Chris Seligman, John Crossingham, and Brendan Canning; Kevin Drew and Andrew Whiteman; and Broken Social Scene performing at Soundscapes in Toronto, 2002. (SC)

You Forgot It In People came out. That was a crazy time for me, because I was flip-flopping between both bands. It was exhausting, but I wasn't complaining — it was amazing.

JASON COLLETT_ The first record [*Feel Good Lost*] was being made when I was doing Radio Monday, and all those guys came and played [the night]: Whitey played it, Millan played it, Haines and Jimmy played it, Kevin played it. I wasn't interested in joining the band at that time because I had my hands full with the family and I was trying to get my own record together. When they were planning their first tour [for *You Forgot It In People*], they had asked me to open for them. They would back me up and then I would play in the band. That tour fell through, but I had way too much fun during the rehearsal.

I COME FROM MORE OF A TRADITIONAL SONGWRITING BACKGROUND, BUT I'M ALWAYS SO IMPRESSED HOW [IN BROKEN SOCIAL SCENE] SONGWRITING IS TURNED ON ITS HEAD.

I come from more of a traditional songwriting background, but I'm always so impressed how [in Broken Social Scene] songwriting is turned on its head. I think a big influence on that process has always been the Do Makes. Originally, Broken Social Scene was just an instrumental thing, and then when vocals were introduced, they were really treated as just another instrument, with stream-of-consciousness lyrics. Lyrics can really be cumbersome, and what's so great about the band is they never let them get in the way. There's an emotive level to what Kevin does that transcends any literal sense. People can relate to the songs on an instinctual, gut level — it's a higher form of communicating, really.

JULIE PENNER_ I had played Jason Collett's CD release show in November 2002, and after that, Kevin started leaving his classic long, rambling messages on my answering machine. At first I didn't know what to make of them. I remember thinking, "Is this guy nuts?" At some point he asked me to play violin for the *You Forgot It In People* CD release at Lula Lounge. I had one practice session with the boys, which was all I needed.

AMY MILLAN_ My first show with Broken Social Scene was at the *You Forgot It In People* CD release party at Lula Lounge. Emily was in L.A., and Feist had moved to Paris. The girls were gone, so Kevin came to me and said, "I need you to be the girl." I was nervous because I knew I was around some incredible musicians, like Charles Spearin and Brendan Canning. I didn't really know the rest of the band as well as I knew Kevin. I had been singing with Emily since I was fifteen, so pulling off the Emily parts wasn't as difficult as [Feist's on] "Almost Crimes," which was a completely different way of singing for me — that firecracker Feist way. It was a really great show, and there was a definite atmosphere of excitement for something new that was going to be big. Then I ended up touring with the group for three years.

K-OS_ I saw Broken Social Scene at Lula Lounge. I don't know if he remembers this, but Kevin and I talked on the phone that week and he told me to come by and, if I felt like it, to join in. I was aware of no buzz, just the music and the audacity of having so many people onstage — you know, the whole Wu-Tang Clan comparison. I kept looking for a place to jump in or do some vocals, but [the show's momentum] was building by itself. I guess it was mostly the music's ultramagnetics that got me, and the nostalgia, which emanated from my high-school years. Everyone in that band reminded me of a close friend in high school that I had lost touch with. That's what appealed to me — the distant familiarity.

***DANKO JONES*_** There was one tour in particular that I came back home from and Brendan was on the cover of *Eye Weekly*, and I was like, "What the hell's going on?" Broken Social Scene had just kind of exploded. Every time we'd come home from Europe — we'd be out there for two months at a time — the only thing I really noticed was that Broken Social Scene's profile was getting bigger and bigger.

***KEVIN DREW⁵*_** When I talked to Lorraine Carpenter of the Montreal *Mirror*, she said, "Toronto is just viewed as a major-label town, but now we see that there are all these great bands coming out." There are all these great bands coming out because the indies are now putting out better music than the majors, and that's the way it's been for the past three years. There are more records coming out now from people involved in this record — my goal is to see a tree in some rock magazine, of who plays with who, showing all these people who lived within thirty-two blocks of each other and all their albums. The music in this town right now is not great — it's wonderful.

Flyer promoting the release of *You Forgot It In People*, 2002. (JPF)

MAJOR LABEL DEBUT